The Cartoon History of Humanism

Copyright © 2016 by Dale DeBakcsy

HUMANIST PRESS

1777 T Street NW, Washington, DC 20009
www.humanistpress.com

Printed book ISBN: 978-0-931779-70-1

Illustrations by Count Dolby von Luckner
Design by Jan Melchior

The Cartoon History of Humanism

VOLUME ONE: ANTIQUITY TO ENLIGHTENMENT

Words by Dale DeBakcsy
Art by Count Dolby von Luckner

HUMANIST PRESS

A TABLE OF CONTENTS

An Introduction is no slight thing where strangers are concerned....

Hello! Perhaps you are an old friend, who has been reading the web column upon which this book is based since its premiere, in which case, firstly, (1) Thanks, Mom, and (2) Welcome back! One difference you'll spot right away is that whereas online I let Dave travel hither and thither through history, the order of this book is strictly chronological. We thought this would make for a more sensible reading experience, but as a result a couple of comics refer to events in chronologically later episodes (specifically, episodes 3 and 8). We beg your magnanimous indulgence.

This might, however, be our first time meeting, in which case an explanation is in order. What follows is not an exhaustive history of worldwide humanism from Greek antiquity through the end of the Enlightenment. It's not even a Greatest Hits of Skeptical Thinkers. We've quite enough of those as it is. Nope, this is a completely idiosyncratic visual waltz through some of my favorite thinkers and doers of the humanist tradition, the only requirement for inclusion being that they did Something extraordinary to expand the intellectual horizons and freedoms of humanity. It includes many of the flatly anti-religious philosophers you'd expect, but also a number of priests, rulers, artists, and theologians who, each in their own way, nudged up the boundaries of human potential.

Friedrich Nietzsche, in *On the Uses and Disadvantages of History for Life,* talks about the different ways that our relation with history affects our engagement with the present. In that essay, he defines the "antiquarian" type, one who plods away, desperately preserving the past at all costs, often to the detriment of the living and evolving present. I try to fight it, but I am absolutely one such, and the choices in this book reflect that basic psychological need. I give you the Archpoet, Arnold of Brescia, Hermann Reimarus, and Isabella d'Este rather than Socrates and Baron d'Holbach because it pains me to think that life stories like theirs might be forgotten by their own intellectual descendants. Those stories are crazy, and foundational, and inspiring, and totally improbable, and deserve as many tellings as we can give them. That's why this comic series exists, and those tales form the wild contours of the historical ride, in a not entirely chronological order, I propose we embark on together now.

Grab your muffler, good badger, for it's a brisk morning to go adventuring.

—Dale DeBakcsy, August 2016, Castro Valley, CA.

Epicurus and the Right to Moderately Party

HI, I'M DAVE. AS A CHILD, I MADE FUN OF A PASSING LOGICAL POSITIVIST, AND SO SHE CURSED ME TO WANDER TIME AND SPACE, CONVERSING WITH HUMANIST PHILOSOPHERS UNTIL I LEARN MY LESSON.

IT HAPPENS.

NEXT UP IS EPICURUS, MATERIALIST SUPREME AND CHAMPION OF PLEASURE. TO GET HIS WISDOM, I NEED TO EARN HIS TRUST.

DON'T WORRY, THOUGH. I GOOGLED HIM AND KNOW *JUST* WHAT TO DO...

EPICURUS! I'M HERE! LET'S GET *DROOOOONK!*

BUT, WHY?

CAUSE, YOU KNOW... PLEASURE... N SUCH.

BUT IS IT PLEASURE IF IT EXCEEDS THE BOUNDS OF REASON? MUSTN'T IT BE BOTH *PRUDENT* AND *HONORABLE?*

I GUESSSS? LISTEN, SO, I SUPPOSE I'LL JUST GO OVER TO ZENO'S, THEN?

THE *STOIC?!*

YEAH, WORD IS THAT THOSE GUYS ARE *CRAZY* FUN.

WHAT?!

JUST SOMETHING I HEARD, UM, *ARISTOTLE* SAY...

THAT HUSSY! MIRIAM, BREAK OUT THE SPECIAL *GUEST* CHEESES! WE'LL SHOW THEM THAT EPICUREANS ARE STILL THE MASTERS OF MODERATE LEISURE!!

"The wise man neither rejects life nor fears death. For living does not offend him, nor does he believe not living to be something bad. And just as he does not unconditionally choose the largest amount of food but the most pleasant food, so he savours not the longest time but the most pleasant."

**– Epicurus,
Letter to Menoeceus**

In 309 BCE, Epicurus settled permanently in an Athens that was the merest twitchy whisper of its former self. The proud democracy that stood resolutely against Persian tyranny and led a coalition against Sparta's power had been broken by the Macedonians in 322 BCE, its political institutions gutted, and its glory never to return. In the wake of these events, new systems of philosophy sprung up, thick skinned collections of pragmatic thought that peeled away the excesses of the Platonists to return Reality to the throne.

This was the age of Hellenistic philosophy, and it is thoroughly gorgeous and delightful, though Christianity's obsession with Plato and Aristotle would all but bury its significance in the ensuing millennia. The three major schools were Epicureanism, Stoicism, and Skepticism, and all of them took as their starting premise that things had gotten Way Out Of Hand under Plato. The revered Athenian's monomania for abstract forms and incorporeal perfections struck the Hellenists as dangerously idealistic, threatening to sacrifice entirely the good of the world as it is in the pursuit of artful fables.

Our guy, Epicurus (341 BCE—270 BCE), was a dedicated materialist and atomist. He held that, when the body dies, nothing survives. We are done, and need to make our peace with that fact. Further, in a move that would have to wait 1900 years for resurrection at the hands of Giordano Bruno (who would then promptly get burned at the hands of the Inquisition for it), he maintained that, to learn about the stuff of the heavens, we need to learn about how things work on Earth and draw parallels. To understand stars and moons and eclipses, we need to understand the nature we have available to us, and not just throw up our hands, call everything in the sky "divine" and start recklessly philosophizing about what it all *ought* to be like.

He also wasn't particularly fond of anything that denigrated our lived experience and perceptions in favor of Realities Beyond. He stressed the importance of each person's different biological makeup, and how that biology might impact how we perceive the world, without then making the Platonic step of saying that because we all perceive reality differently, we should abandon trust in mere perception. Rather, Epicurus hotly maintained, we need to learn to respect the individuality of perception, the reality of the mental event itself. Even when hallucinating, something very real is happening to our bodies, an event that deserves investigation, though the objects of the hallucination don't "exist" out in the world in the ordinary sense. He was a psychologist in an age of idealists.

But, of course we know him as "The Pleasure Guy," or "Dr. Hedonism," or "Johnny Orgy." And it is certainly true that he maintained that the pleasures of humanity were important and that friendship was the central fact of pleasant existence. But his writings, or the meager scraps that survive of his hundreds of volumes, are very explicit in their warnings against excess. Excess carries with it the stuff of pain and cuts off the nurturing flow of those things that give us everyday contentment. Epicurus himself considered "a pot of cheese" to be a grand indulgence, a cup of diluted wine entirely sufficient, and was probably a vegetarian to boot.

Shortly after the age of Hellenism, humanism would be forced underground, only daring to show itself when draped in a costume of religious observance that worked at cross purposes to its message. But here, in this tenuous blip between the fall of classical Greece and the emergence of world Christianity, humans were considering their humanity and, in a glorious moment too wonderful to last, deemed it to be enough.

NOTES ON THE COMIC

Epicurus, as far as we know, did not have a wife. If he did, she would not have been called Miriam. But somehow, the idea of bringing out the "guest cheeses" seemed incomplete to me unless somebody named Miriam was involved somehow. Also, the overlap between the lives of Aristotle and Epicurus was only about twenty years, so Aristotle would have been long dead by the time Epicurus was this old.

Lucretius: The MacGyver of Natural Philosophy

HEY LUCRETIUS, LOOKS LIKE YOU'RE PONDERING...

I WAS JUST THINKING HOW, IN A VACUUM, ALL BODIES MUST FALL AT THE SAME RATE REGARDLESS OF MASS.

PSH... SO YOU ANTICIPATED GALILEO... LUCKY GUESS.

... AND THAT THE VISIBLE MOTIONS OF MINISCULE PARTICLES ARE CAUSED BY UNOBSERVABLE ATOMIC JOSTLING.

WHICH IS EINSTEIN'S ACCOUNT OF BROWNIAN MOTION.

... AND THAT SENSATION IS A PHYSICAL PROCESS TRIGGERED BY THE RELEASE OF TINY PRIMER MOLECULES WHICH CREATE A MENTAL CHAIN REACTION...

DUDE, YOU JUST DESCRIBED *NEURO-TRANSMITTERS*.

... AND THAT THE UNIVERSE WAS CREATED BY NATURAL PROCESSES AND TENDS TOWARDS DISORDER.

THAT'S THE SECOND LAW OF THERMODYNAMICS. YOU'RE KIND OF FREAKING ME OUT, LUCRETIUS.

...AND...

STOP! CAN'T YOU JUST SAY SOME QUAINTLY WRONG BIT OF ANTIQUE SCIENTIFIC WISDOM SO I CAN GO BACK TO FEELING WAY SMUG AND SUPERIOR?

UMMM... LIONS ARE AFRAID OF ROOSTERS BECAUSE THEY HAVE CHICKEN-SHAPED PORES IN THEIR EYEBALLS?

AHHH YEAH. *THAT'S* THE STUFF.

Lucretius is the keystone of Materialism, its prime example of how staggeringly far a single mind can go in understanding the universe aided by nothing but the proposition that everything is composed of atoms. His masterpiece, *De Rerum Natura*, published over *two thousand* years ago, is an astonishing encapsulation of prescient hyper-modern insights into the physical world. From genetics to cosmology, optics to neuroscience, Lucretius's ideas are correct freakishly often, explainable only under the hypothesis that (1) Lucretius was a Time Lord or (2) a little bit of materialism unencumbered by the need for theogonic consistency goes a long way indeed.

We know shockingly little about the man whose book was to become a rallying point for early modern atomism and a rich wellspring for considering its consequences. We know that, like his role model and inspiration, Epicurus, he lived in a time of tectonic civilizational change. Born 100 BCE-ish, Lucretius experienced the last days of the Roman Republic and died on the very eve of the empire around 55 BCE. During that time, two Roman generals, Marius and Sulla, broke the back of the republic with their constant wrangling for power, each establishing in turn a rule more tyrannical than the last. Political enemies were executed in droves on the streets of Rome as the vaunted purveyors of Roman religion and justice stood impotently by.

Little wonder, then, that a return to the evenhanded realism of Epicurus proved so popular. In a world so markedly capricious, maintaining a belief in the rule of benevolent gods was not merely foolish, but harmful. In his masterpiece, before he gets down to the business of explaining Life, The Universe, and Everything, Lucretius makes it his first priority to clear away the inherited religious detritus of the Greek and Roman systems and to remind us of the violence to which religious belief incites men:

"Remember how at Aulis the altar of the Virgin Goddess was foully stained with the blood of Iphigenia … struck dumb with terror, she sank on her knees to the ground…. It was her fate in the very hour of marriage to fall a sinless victim to a sinful rite, slaughtered to her greater grief by a father's hand, so that a fleet might sail under happy auspices. Such are the heights of wickedness to which men are driven by religion."

He then sits back, proposes the idea that everything we know is the result of entirely natural processes driven by the combination and recombination of elemental atoms, and treats us to a Neil deGrasse Tyson-worthy tour through the now explainable mysteries of the cosmos and the human mind. The book is an accomplishment which has only grown more staggering with the passing of time, as ideas which were scoffed away as unworthy in the eighteenth century have since gained vindication from an age able to physically probe the regions he touched with his powerful sense of imaginative rigor. Here is a modest sampling of what he was able to conclude from the vantage point of basic atomism:

1 The sun is the result of the chance combining of atoms over time, arising out of a natural accumulation, and having an inevitable and fixed end. It is not a deity, not even eternal, but just another natural object that must be constantly diminishing from radiation. The earth, also, is a natural object, with a definite and irrevocable end.

2 There is a special material substance passed on to children which has within it contributions not only from the mother and father, but from previous relatives as well, the resultant child being determined by the particular ancestral mixture passed on from each parent. So, inheritance is determined by a random remixing of traits from multiple generations encoded on some physical medium…so, meiotic crossing over and DNA.

3 New organs and physical variations arise and are kept based on their usefulness. We weren't created with eyes for the express purpose of seeing, but rather, an eye-like thing occurring throughout the random combinations of living forms, it created the possibility of sight, which was useful. It's tantalizingly on the verge of our notion of genetic mutation as the motivator of evolutionary change, and a rebuttal of intelligent design two thousand years before the fact.

4 The speed of light must be slower in more dense media due to interference effects, and opacity is the result of coherent images being scattered by a non-uniform surface. Mirror images are the results of reflecting particles, and how far "into" the mirror they appear is determined by an act of physical/mental calculation. Granted, Lucretius thinks the act of computation is triggered by the amount of air a traveling image particle pushes in front of it, rather than the straight-line computation model we've since discovered. But still, a lot of the basic structures are there.

5 Air is a fluid, and must be treated as such in all questions of falling bodies. Different objects fall at different rates because of the impact of air particles on the falling body, but in a vacuum, all objects should fall at the same rate, regardless of weight. That's Galileo.

6 Sensory motions and reactions are triggered by incredibly small particles which create a cascading chain reaction amongst larger masses of atoms to produce sensation. Lacking our vocabulary of nerves and nerve-triggering neurotransmitters, Lucretius nevertheless once again picked up on some of the salient physical details of sensation—that a miniscule initial physical reaction to a stimulus has to be appropriately amplified through intermediary circuitry, and that somewhere in the automatic processing of that signal lies our sensation of that stimulus.

7 "It is in the highest degree unlikely that this earth and sky is the only one to have been created and that all those particles of matter outside are accomplishing nothing. This follows from the fact that our world has been made by nature through spontaneous and casual collision and the multifarious, accidental, random and purposeless congregation and coalescence of atoms whose suddenly formed combinations could serve on each occasion as the starting point of substantial fabrics—earth and sea and sky and the races of living creatures. On every ground, therefore, you must admit that there exists elsewhere other congeries of matter similar to this one which the ether clasps in ardent embrace." Boom.

Sure, there are parts of *De Rerum Natura* which are just plain wrong. Though he annihilates with devastating cleverness the ancient idea that the whole universe must be made of one of the four classical substances (fire, for example, if you believe Heraclitus), those substances still figure prominently in a number of his explanations. But even some of his seeming absurdities, like the rooster-shaped eyeball pores in our comic, hold at their core something very powerful and true. What he was giving utterance to is the idea that we now recognize as true: that molecular shape has a crucial role in how that molecule functions. Bend a protein one way, and it does one job, bend it another, and it does something completely different. Lucretius's obsession with hypothesizing about the role that atom shape plays, which struck later chemists as comical, was actually a good deal closer to the mark than most chemistry before the mid-twentieth century was capable of realizing.

Our sniggering was premature, as sniggering often is. Of course, the grand tragedy is that this shimmering moment of potential was produced on the doorstep of Christian cosmological hegemony. If one mind, starting from materialist principles, was able to produce all of those astonishing insights within the span of forty-five short years, what might a whole continent have accomplished in the millennium and a half it took us to allow ourselves the pleasure of his philosophical company again?

Such is the standard lament, but remember that the Greeks and Romans were not experimental people. They were astounding in their ability to take a premise to its logical conclusions, and where the initial premise was good, as it was with Lucretius, the end results were brilliant. But the scientific method of devising test conditions to verify hypotheses is a necessary thing to regular and reliable progress, and who is to say that the daft fumbling of medieval Aristotelianism wasn't exactly the thing that we needed to shock us into such a radically rigorous way of searching for knowledge? Perhaps the poetry of Lucretius was too alluring an intellectual diet to spark such a fundamental departure in scientific thought.

Ultimately, Lucretius stands at the zenith of ancient materialism, and the traditional story goes that our humanist thread doesn't get picked up again until perhaps the fifteenth century. But, as Mikhail Bulgakov noted in a different time of darkness, "Manuscripts don't burn," and our next few figures represent startling returns to the best classical traditions during the most unpromising of times. So, let us enter, if we dare, the Dark Ages!

Cicero: Classical Skepticism on the Brink of Empire

For seventeen hundred years, if you did not have Cicero (106—43 BCE) on your bookshelf, you simply did not intellectually count. The elegance of his Latin was so potent that, in the sixteenth century, a millennium and a half after his death, there was an entire movement which had as its central proposition that Ciceronian language should be declared the ultimate in verbal expression, and all advances beyond its conventions outlawed. His was the voice that communicated Greek philosophy to the Roman world and Middle Ages, and provided a model of religious and philosophical skepticism so respectable and revered that the most ardent Christians couldn't bring themselves to send him to hell, but rather carved out a special place in purgatory for antiquity's most eloquent doubter.

Cicero was one of the very few philosophers in the Western tradition who was also actively engaged in shaping public policy. He was as important in the abstract realm as in the political, and had to deal with ethical practicalities that most philosophers airily brush away from the comfort of their metaphysical systems. Aquinas never had to vote on a land redistribution measure. Abelard never had to make a decision between preserving an individual's life and preventing civil war. Cicero regularly did, and the particular greyness of those situations colored his philosophy, preventing him from subscribing to easy theoretical imperatives which existed only on paper.

His whole life was a challenge to the traditional notion of how philosophy and religion were to be done. Like Bertolt Brecht during a later age, he thought it was irresponsible for a human being not to be politically engaged, that the worst crime was social apathy. As humans, our first duty is to each other and to the maintenance of the dreadfully fragile thing we call our government. To say that politics is too dirty a concern to involve yourself in is nothing more than to say you consider your own ethereal purity more important than the good of your fellow citizens, and that is something of which to be ashamed rather than proud.

He lived during the worst of times. The Roman Republic, which had stood and expanded steadily for seven centuries, was in a state of lingering governmental paralysis, as elite senators jealously guarded their privileges in the face of an urban population united behind tribunes whose power of veto effectively guaranteed gridlock and corruption as the unvarying way of things. When he was an adolescent, he watched Sulla and Marius march armies on Rome in a bloody civil war that gutted the senatorial class in an orgy of vengeful executions. Armies were determining legislative policy, and organized street terror was recognized as the most effective way of pushing policies through the Senate.

The Senate's incompetence at dealing with the threats of Sulla and Marius, and the chaos and tragedy that followed in the wake of that rudderlessness formed the crucial memories of not only Cicero, but Pompey and Caesar, Brutus and Antony, all of whom would have their share at desperately and drastically changing the way Rome functioned. While most of the future revolutionaries found places in the army, Cicero took up work as an advocate, using his phenomenal oratorical skill and conscientious thoroughness to win several important cases against long odds. In a sliver of time he'd become the most famous orator of his age and then, just as suddenly, he left Rome to go on a philosophical tour of Greece, placing himself at the feet of the greatest thinkers and orators of each tradition in a grand attempt to hone his own mind and technique. He devoured the works of the great Attic tradition and perfected the style that would soon change the course of Rome and very nearly save the republic from the clutches of empire.

Back at Rome, he enjoyed every elation of success and shudder of ill-fortune that public life has to offer. He was lauded as an ethical and competent administrator in Sicily, and wildly cheered as a consul (the highest administrative post of ancient Rome) when he foiled the Catilinarian conspiracy against the state. But he was also exiled, his beloved villas ransacked and destroyed, and his property confiscated, when his enemies in turn rose to power. His oratory was unbeatable, but his first books, which heaped lavish self-praise on his abilities as a consul, were ruthlessly and deservedly mocked by the literate public.

When Julius Caesar crossed the Rubicon, Cicero sided with the Senate. In Spain, Egypt, Africa, and Greece, Caesar was triumphant, while Cicero, as one of the few senators of any importance left, was assiduously courted to make his peace with the unstoppable general and so lend legitimacy to the new regime. Over the next six years, Cicero engaged in the most dangerous game, playing all sides at once in a desperate attempt to save the last vestiges of the old republic and its institutions. When Caesar was assassinated, Cicero championed the cause of Julius's declared heir, Octavian, believing the young lad to be as thoroughly dedicated to the restoration of the republic as he declared. At the height of his power, Cicero led the Senate in valiantly resisting the dictatorial trends of Marc

Antony, pushing him into exile and nearly into total defeat until Octavian saw his moment, switched loyalties, and joined with Antony to restore Caesar's order. As an offering to Antony, Octavian surrendered the life of the man who had been his mentor and friend.

A death warrant was put out for Cicero, and a team of professional bounty hunters soon caught up with him as he attempted to escape to Greece. With stoic resolve, he pulled back his collar, stuck out his neck, and told them to get about their business of ending his life. His hands and head were lopped off and brought back to Rome to Antony's great joy, Octavian's sorrow, and Rome's permanent detriment.

But he had left behind more than a political legacy. During the last decade of his life, he wrote books with a frenzy approaching madness. These included towering summaries of all the schools of Greek thought, much of which we still only know about because Cicero was so good as to write it down for us. There were also treatises on oratory, statesmanship, and the phenomenon of grief, all of which were read and commented upon with rapt attention by Europe's intellectual elite for centuries. For the humanist, the most important of this literary legacy is doubtlessly his *On the Nature of the Gods* (45 BCE), a work which contains all of the contemporary arguments as to the existence and nature of the gods, and provides devastating rebuttals of each, all in the name of a reasonable skepticism which admits the limits of what humans can meaningfully talk about.

It's ostensibly a dialogue, but it is mainly a series of set speeches and rebuttals between an Epicurean, a Stoic, and a skeptic who is essentially Cicero's stand-in. The Epicurean and Stoic are both given

their chances to argue (a) that gods exist, (b) what those gods are like, and (c) what those gods do with themselves. Their positions are, essentially, those that we still hear today offered by Christians and other theists. The Goldilocks argument, the First Cause argument, the All Men Believe It argument, the Moral Source argument, several variations on the ontological argument, all trotted forth in words that the most extreme Southern Baptist would feel entirely at home uttering, and all smashed utterly by the common sense of Ciceronian skepticism. By the end of the book, nothing is definitively said about the gods except that everything asserted so far by philosophy and religion is almost definitely wrong.

Active gods and retiring gods, gods that are the world and that are utterly other to it, gods that listen to men and those who are indifferent to them, every shade of god offered up is shown as a tissue of contradictions supported by an unwise abundance of faith in linguistic devices and common assent. In addition, we are treated to the following anecdote about a famous Greek atheist which might have claim to be the first story told in the Western tradition where a nonbeliever is the good guy:

Good men have sometimes success. They have so; but we cannot, with any show of reason, attribute that success to the Gods. Diagoras, who is called the atheist, being at Samothrace, one of his friends showed him several pictures of people who had endured very dangerous storms; "See," says he, "You who denies a Providence, how many have been saved by their prayers to the Gods." "Ay," says Diagoras, "I see those who were saved, but where are those painted who were shipwrecked?"

At another time, he himself was in a storm, when the sailors, being greatly alarmed, told him they justly deserved that misfortune for admitting him into their ship; when he, pointing to other ships under like distress, asked them "if they believed Diagoras was also aboard those ships?"

Those are still both pretty solid slams, in a book teeming with wry Ciceronian humor in the face of philosophico-linguistic posturing. We see in this slim book how devastating an opponent Cicero could be on the debate floor, and why a man such as Antony took such particular joy in his removal from Roman public life. Reading his oratory might no longer be part of our common cultural practice, but for humanists seeking an example of philosophy engaging with the real world, and of skepticism's deep ancestry, an evening alone with Cicero will always be a fruitful thing.

FURTHER READING

Anthony Everitt's *Cicero: The Life and Times of Rome's Greatest Politician* (2001) is a very good introduction to Cicero's life, wittily written and easily available. Its focus is definitely, as the title implies, on Cicero the politician rather than Cicero the thinker, and his written work is disposed of more or less in a single chapter, while his role in the ongoing Civil Wars is examined in minute detail. For Cicero the thinker there's really no current substitute for his own works. Because half of the experience of Cicero is in his beautiful Latin phrasing, this is one of those cases where reading in English is to miss a large chunk of his work's impact. If you pick up the Loeb edition of *On the Nature of the Gods*, you can enjoy both the original and H. Rackham's English translation of it on facing pages. Loeb editions are great resources and look lovely on a shelf, but they're also pricey, even for used copies, so if you want just English, you can pick up C.D. Yonge's old 1877 translation on your favorite electronic device for one or two dollars. Hot tip: If you're super familiar with ancient Greek philosophy, you'll probably enjoy the depth of presentation that Cicero gives to the Epicurean and Stoic positions. If not, and you just want to watch him dismantle terrible religious arguments, skip straight to the Cotta sections and enjoy!

Arnold of Brescia: The Man So Important You've Never Heard of Him

ROME, 1151.

AND THAT IS WHY NO MONK, NO BISHOP, NO POPE SHOULD WIELD TEMPORAL POWER! FOR DEMOCRACY AND THE ROMAN COMMUNE!

HURRAH!

RASSIN!

THAT'S A GOODA SPEECH!

THIS IS PRETTY RADICAL STUFF, ARNOLD. HOW DO YOU KNOW IT WILL WORK?

WE DID IT IN LOMBARDY!

WITH AN INVESTED, POLITICALLY SAVVY, AND EXTENSIVE MERCHANT CLASS...

PRECISELY!

WHICH YOU DON'T HAVE HERE IN ROME.

GOSH, WE *DON'T.* IS THAT BAD?

LEAP-FROGGING SOCIO-ECONOMIC STAGES DOESN'T HAVE A **GREAT** TRACK RECORD, NO.

BUT, WE'LL APPEAL TO THE EMPEROR! *SURELY* HE'LL COME TO OUR AID!

BECAUSE MEDIEVAL EMPERORS FAMOUSLY *LOVE* INDEPENDENT CITY REPUBLICS.

EXACTLY!

OH, YOU POOR, BEAUTIFUL, NAIVE MAN...

Sometimes, it's good to be da pope. The twelfth century, however, was not one of those times. Antipopes, uppity monarchs, and failed Crusades all took their toll on a papacy ever more at a loss to explain just how its marked addiction to opulence helped Jesus's plan for humanity. The greatest indignity, however, came at the hands of the Roman people who, tired of the pope's exercise of governmental and judicial power, threw him out of Rome in 1144 to establish a democratic commune. A holy bindlestiff trudging about Italy for a decade trying to justify his existence to whatever monarch might lend him a hand in retaking his city, the pope was an flickering shade desperately seeking relevance.

And the man who contributed most to making him that way was Arnold of Brescia. Executed in 1155 at the hands of an indifferent emperor, vengeful pope, and treacherous senate, the Roman Curia was so worried about his body becoming a focal point for further revolution that it ordered him cremated and his ashes flung into the Tiber River. The church hoped to cast his memory alike with his remains to the waters, to be dissipated and ultimately forgotten, and they succeeded. For most people today, he is a footnote of a footnote, in spite of the fact that he came within an imperial nod of establishing the Reformation four hundred years ahead of its time.

He was born sometime between 1090 and 1105 in the Lombard town of Brescia. The city was, at the time, second only to Milan in terms of economic importance and political consciousness. Thriving merchant and artisan classes crackled with new ideas for self-governance and, in the jumble following the dissolution of the Carolingian Empire, saw their chance to grab power. The only thing that stood in their way were the bishops, holders of immense wealth and temporal authority, who had astutely been filling the power vacuum.

The contest between the burgeoning middle class and the bishops came to a head in 1138 when Bishop Manfred fled Brescia for Rome in a desperate attempt to plea for papal help in re-establishing his authority. For three years prior to that, the townsmen had been slowly chipping away at the bishop's power base, and at first Arnold wasn't sure whose side to join. He had spent a decade studying with Peter Abelard, whose intellectual, analytic approach toward religion couldn't have been more different from Arnold's unlikely mixture of asceticism and demagoguery. And yet, the two men became fast friends, and when it was Abelard's time to go on trial for heresy in 1141, Arnold of Brescia stood by his side.

Because Arnold left no writings, it is hard to entirely pin down what he learned from Abelard beyond a general principle of the necessity to confront authority whenever it errs. While Abelard criticized the intellectual failings of mystical theology, Arnold attacked the church's political power. In a time when the church owned sprawling tracts of land, controlled vast hoards of wealth, launched armies to achieve its political goals, and claimed for itself an increasing share of judicial authority, Arnold argued for a complete return to a purely spiritual role. Simony and land ownership had corrupted the heart of Christianity's purpose, and distracted it from its role in alleviating the suffering of the common folk. Nothing would be right until the church returned its holdings to the people and renounced its role in mediating terrestrial affairs.

These were the ideas he possessed when returning to Brescia on the eve of its revolution against the bishops. Like everything in medieval history, the situation was a complicated brew of regional, religious, economic, and social factors that have become polarized and cartoonishly simplified in the retelling. The fact was that the bishops were trying to reform some of the very evils that Arnold complained of, while the revolutionaries were a mixture of honest democrats and self-serving low-level priests trying to foil the bishops' plans. Who Arnold should ally with was therefore not an easy matter, but ultimately, the pull of popular justice couldn't be denied, and Arnold fell in with the nascent commune and thereby sealed his fate.

His ability as a speaker soon brought him to the head of the movement and, in 1139, when the pope finally spoke out against Brescia's rebellion, Arnold was singled out for exile. The bishop returned bearing the pope's command, and the Brescia commune, a grand experiment in self-government that was to be repeated many times over the Lombard landscape, crumbled.

Arnold wandered a while after that, returning to the historical record at Abelard's final trial for heresy. Their joint appearance did neither any good, unfortunately. The acid-tongued Bernard of Clairvaux (later Saint Bernard, since nothing so betokens a saint as persistent and consuming vindictiveness wed to power) used Arnold's bad political reputation to undermine Abelard's position by association, ultimately securing Abelard's final censure. While for Arnold, being seen in public on Abelard's side made him an object of sustained interest to Bernard, who kept tabs ever afterwards on the wandering exile's movements. The most influential clergyman of his day, Bernard made sure to write to anybody offering Arnold protection, warning them against endangering their own position in the church by harboring such a viper.

While Arnold was in exile, Rome was taking its first, somewhat inglorious, steps to self-governance. To understand what happened, you have to know that the neighboring cities of Rome and Tivoli did not like each other particularly much. Tivoli supported the antipope Anacletus while the Romans, at least until they kicked him out, supported Innocent II. Taking the whole rebellion against authority thing a step fur-

ther, the Tivolese rejected Rome's political authority over them and, when Rome tried to subdue the upstart city by force in 1142, the townsmen's staunch defense thoroughly defeated and humiliated the Roman forces.

So, Rome being Rome, they tried attacking again the next year, and this time were successful. The Roman people demanded that Tivoli be burnt to the ground, but the pope instead negotiated a relatively benign treaty restoring the peace. The Romans, denied their bloody vengeance, arose *en masse* and set up a government of their own.

Innocent was left to sulk impotently in the Lateran and died soon thereafter. His

successor reigned for less than a year and didn't manage much, which brought Lucius II to papal power. Forging an alliance with the king of Sicily, he formed an army to retake Rome, and attacked the city in 1145.

And failed.

And got hit in the head by a rock.

And died.

His replacement, Eugene III, was a modest man who lived an honest life, and didn't like to solve things by violence if it could be avoided. All of which made him startlingly unique among the role-call of medieval popes, and also particularly well-suited to dealing with the Roman commune. Arnold appealed to him for forgiveness and was granted it by the gentle Eugene. Thereupon, Arnold made his way to Rome just as Eugene was making a deal with the commune to split power between the papal officials and the democratically elected senators.

The era of good feelings was not meant to last, however. In 1146 Eugene was cast out of Rome, and Arnold was at the head of the movement against him. Inveighing against the corrupting military and economic might of the papacy, he inspired the city to continue its resistance and seek protection from foreign rulers against the pope's return.

However, the brisk competence in governing that was natural to the savvy citizens of Lombardy was utterly lacking among the Romans. Without a sizeable artisan class, perpetually unsure of what they wanted to accomplish, the movement was ever in danger of coming to tatters. That it lasted as long as it did was due mainly to the eloquence of Arnold, the hope of imperial support, and a convenient distraction.

For, it turned out, Bernard of Clairvaux was all hot and bothered after the fall of

Edessa to start up a new Crusade, and used his influence to ignite a groundswell of support for the idea. Eugene, then, instead of concentrating on regaining his control of Rome, had to tour through Europe, organizing the grand effort that would ultimately lead to the fantastically underwhelming (at least on the Eastern front) Second Crusade. Thus tied up, the Commune had some years of breathing space to experiment with democratic government.

Finally able to devote his attention to the rather embarrassing matter of not being the ruler of his own spiritual capital, the pope made peace again in 1149, but then fled, again, in 1150. Eugene's way of doing things, charming as it was, clearly was not getting the job done.

That's when Nicholas Breakspear showed up.

Breakspear was every bit as badass as somebody with the last name of Breakspear ought to be. When he became pope in 1154, he made it known that he was officially DONE with this Commune nonsense. For the first time in history, he placed the whole city of Rome under interdiction on the eve of Easter, meaning that no religious ceremonies could be performed there. The Roman people, who believed sternly that disaster would befall the city if Easter Mass were to be given a miss that year, begged him to return. Meanwhile, Breakspear had invited Frederick Barbarossa to march into Italy with his armies and restore order. Cutting a path of terror through Lombardy, Frederick and his Germans finally arrived at Rome and proceeded to slaughter its citizenry. The Commune was finished, Frederick was made an emperor, and Breakspear entered history as Pope Adrian IV, protector of the faith.

The city, which had agreed to protect Arnold no matter what might happen, promptly turned on him when Adrian asked for the surrender of their most famous revolutionary. Arnold managed to escape, but not for long. Adrian asked Barbarossa to handle the matter of executing Arnold, because it was perfectly seemly for popes to *order* the murder of a human being, or a city, just not to carry it out themselves.

Arnold was executed by hanging in 1155 at an unknown location outside of Rome, his ashes cast into the Tiber as per orders. Though "Arnoldists" pop up in papal correspondence from time to time, and though the Roman senate continued to exist for another half century on paper, the movement and the ideas that motivated it were done.

Had Emperor Conrad responded to Rome's pleas for protection, or had his successor Frederick Barbarossa sided with the city instead of the pope, it all might have gone so much differently. The destruction of the pope's political authority and the ascendance of private spirituality over public spectacle might have brought a proto-Reformation to Europe in the twelfth century, and perhaps (oh, let's be thoroughly irresponsible as sober academics, shall we?) a quasi-Enlightenment in the fourteenth. Where would we be, as a world society, had Arnold's wedge in papal power been driven home under the weight of the Hohenstaufens' political support?

It's tempting, and a little heartbreaking, to speculate. As it stands, he failed, utterly, at forcing the papacy to reevaluate its powers and privileges. But then, so did the papacy fail, to use the lesson of the Commune to make itself a less self-contradictory institution and, on a smaller scale, to entirely silence the story of the slightly mad Lombard who, with a simple but persistent call to humility and charity, nearly upset one thousand years of institutional inertia.

FURTHER READING

Arnold of Brescia is mainly somebody you read about in passing in books devoted to other people. The main source for anybody interested is still George Greenaway's 1931 *Arnold of Brescia*, now out of print. Since then, no major biography has appeared in English. If, however, you speak German, you're in a bit better luck. Martina Kleinau's recent *Arnold von Brescia: Reformer oder Ketzer?* is readily available in print and electronic formats and has a very Greenaway perspective to it. Arnold left behind no writings, but if you get the Greenaway, it includes a chapter on all of the original sources we have available which talk about his ideas and life.

One Nun Against God: The Human Tragedy of Héloïse d'Argenteuil

"O vows! O convent! I have not lost my humanity under your inexorable discipline! You have not made me marble by changing my habit."

So, you had this boyfriend. He was a divinity student, which was weird, but you fell in love with him anyway. Ridiculously, stupidly in love, and you got pregnant. Ordinarily, that's fine, but this happened to be the twelfth century, so you got married. Your family was outraged by the whole scandalous affair, dealt with your husband in an appropriately medieval fashion, and then shut you up in a convent.

Now, what do you do with the rest of your life?

For most women of the time, there wasn't much recourse but to sit in the nunnery and await death while slowly convincing themselves somehow in the ultimate goodness of God's mysterious plan. But for one, who happened to be one of the most learned scholars of her age, a voice was given to speak out against the cruelties of the convent and for the embracing of pure, human emotion. She was Héloïse d'Argenteuil (1100?-1164), famous now merely as half of the tragic lover's pair, Héloïse and Abelard, but in her few surviving letters a powerful and challenging mind gleams forth, ready to challenge God himself if need be in pursuit of the personal attachments of our merely mortal life.

We know little of her origins. When Abelard met her, she was living with her "uncle," a Notre Dame canon by the name of Fulbert who could very well have been her father. She was perhaps in her early twenties when Abelard entered her life, and already renowned across France for the depth of her learning and insight. She knew Hebrew, Greek, and Latin fluently and was deeply acquainted with the philosophical works of antiquity, particularly the Stoic tradition. Interestingly, she was among the last women in Europe to be allowed such a level of learning, as after the twelfth century, the Catholic Church reasserted its grasping stewardship of female personal development, taking particular aim at eliminating the grotesque affront of the female Intellectual. It would take three hundred years for women of Héloïse's education to be a semi-common presence in Europe again.

Abelard was, at the time, and pretty much at every time before and after, a cocky logician who thought that every woman loved him and every man stood in smoldering envy of his argumentative skills. His routine was to roam from one learned academy to the next, challenge the reigning lecturer, piss everybody off, and then flee before the consequences became dire. Looking past all of his overwrought egotism, however, one has to admit that he was indeed a startling and original thinker. His books were banned twice by Rome, and one of them, *Sic et Non,* had the temerity to carefully seek out and present all of the myriad instances of church fathers asserting diametrically opposed things about the big questions in religion. He claimed it was to help develop a higher logic that unified all of the clearly contradictory opinions of the past, but the end result was a catalogue detailing with excruciating clarity the absurd logical knots at the heart of Christianity.

He fell in love with Héloïse's mind, and she with his (he was also apparently something of a looker, though on the stout side, and a musician to boot), and he somewhat brilliantly found a way to get her "uncle" to agree to his being her tutor. This gave the young lovers ample opportunity to have all manner of hot-hot medieval forbidden sex, and Héloïse soon found herself with child. Abelard proposed that they had to get married, but Héloïse resisted. According to Abelard's self-serving account in the *Historia Calamitatum*, it was because she didn't want to get in the way of his astounding career as a theologian. In her own letter to him, however, she points out a separate motive. "I was very unwilling to be necessitated to love always a man who, perhaps, would not always love me," she pragmatically assessed, knowing Abelard's reputation as a somewhat inconstant lover. She wanted to love him freely rather than be tied to a dubious relationship for the sake of societal convention. "Though I knew the name of Wife was honourable in the world, and holy in religion, yet the name of your mistress had greater charms, because it was more free."

Let me reiterate that this was the *twelfth century*, and here was a woman essentially arguing that her reproductive fate oughtn't dictate her personal freedom. It is an almost inconceivable leap forward in the concept of female agency, and it is far from the only such instance in the few letters of Héloïse that we possess. Raised on a steady diet of Seneca and other philosophers of antiquity, she had an instinctual and profound respect for the dignity of human freedom and passion, broken eventually only after decades of isolation and Abelard's studied cruelty.

As always, Abelard got his way, and the couple married. Héloïse's family, however, was outraged by Abelard's behavior subsequent to the wedding and decided that the only way to finally solve the problem was to jump him in his sleep and castrate him.

So, that happened.

Abelard, emasculated, forced Héloïse into a convent out of jealousy. If he couldn't have her, then nobody could. And she agreed, again, though every fiber of her person shrieked against the act. "It was your command only," she wrote to him years later, "and not a sincere vocation, as is imagined, that shut me up in these cloisters. I fought to give you ease, and not to sanctify myself."

"I am here, I confess, a sinner, but one who, far from weeping for her sins, weeps only for her lover; far from abhorring her crimes, endeavours only to add to them; and who, with a weakness unbecoming the state I am in, please myself continually with the remembrance of past actions, when it is impossible to renew them."

In Abelard's responses, these blasphemies earn his full reproach, and he continually urges her to accept her fate and give herself up to the pain of existence, to "take the part of God against herself."

He describes their love as an evil that must be replaced by penitence and silent service. She, however, evaluates the measure of man's life with an irresistible bittersweet grace: "If there is anything which may properly be called happiness on Earth, I am persuaded it is the union of two persons who love each other with perfect liberty, who are united by a secret inclination, and satisfied with each other's merit." Or, "What cannot letters inspire? They have souls; they can speak; they have in them all that force which expresses the transports of the heart; they have all the fire of our passions; they can raise them as much as if the persons themselves were present; they have all the softness and delicacy of speech, and

sometimes a boldness of expression even beyond it."

Héloïse, trapped in a cloister against her choosing, reflecting on the happiness of human interaction, and the primacy of liberty in matters of the heart and the head, was becoming entirely too radical for Abelard's taste. After a serious illness weakened her resolve to resist her imposed life, he struck, and hard. He conjured God Almighty, enraged at her resistance to His Plan.

"Provoked at your contempt and ingratitude, God will turn his love into anger, and make you feel his vengeance. How will you sustain his presence when you shall stand before his tribunal? He will reproach you for having despised his grace; he will represent to you his sufferings for you. What answer can you make? He will then be implacable. He will say to you, 'Go, proud creature, dwell in everlasting flames…. Go, wretch, and take the portion of the retrobates.'"

And with that, Abelard signs off the last personal letter he ever sent Héloïse. He accused her of interfering with his salvation, and knew that he was interfering with hers, and refused to correspond further about anything but professional matters. The woman who once wrote, "I am no longer ashamed that my passion has had no bounds," was battered at last into obedient compliance. She wrote theological questions to him, and he answered, and that was all. Abelard died in 1142 and Héloïse lived on until 1164 as the head of a cloister founded by Abelard. She was adored by her charges and by Abelard's students, who saw in her a last connection to their master's sparkling wit and knowledge. Whether she still carried that ember of resistance deep inside her we can't know, but in that tragically small pile of letters we can see a fierce and confident spirit

throwing out a challenge to society and God on behalf of her love and freedom, an example of defiance in the name of humanity so touching and powerful that its like would not be allowed again for centuries.

FURTHER READING

Héloïse's letters are widely available, in both Latin and English translation. There are fewer than a half dozen personal letters between Abelard and Héloïse, with a few more letters about nunnery business beyond those. The latter make for quite tragic reading, as you watch Héloïse gut herself of anything smacking of her former, lustrous humanity in order to keep up any kind of communication with Abelard.
gutenberg.org files/35977/
35977-h/35977-h.htm

Peter Abelard: How to Not Make Friends and Yet Influence People

CLUNY, 1141.

HEY, ABELARD, WHAT'S UP?

WELL, I'VE BEEN CONVICTED OF HERESY, *AGAIN.*

WHAT?! BUT YOU'RE SO DREAMY!

I KNOW! BUT THEY INSISTED THAT MY PRINCIPLE OF USING LOGICAL DIALECTICS TO INVESTIGATE RELIGIOUS IDEAS IS DANGEROUS TO THE CHURCH!

HMM. SO, HOW DO YOU MAKE, LIKE, THE TRINITY, REASONABLE AND LOGICAL?

EASY! BY ANALOGY WITH A SEAL!

ARP ARP?

NO, A WAX SEAL!

THE FATHER, HE'S THE WAX, AND THE SON, HE'S THE *IMPRINT* IN THE WAX!

AND THE GHOSTIE?

MAYBE - THE METAL THING YOU PRESS INTO THE WAX? OR, NO, WAIT, THE *CONCEPT* OF THE METAL THING - THAT MAKES IT MORE GREEK!

IT'SSSS... NOT EXACTLY AIRTIGHT, ABELARD.

OKAY, HOW ABOUT THIS? IT'S LIKE A DONKEY TRAIN, AND THE FATHER...

There are, scattered throughout history, a few characters of such peculiar and innate humanity that, no matter how hard they consciously tried to strengthen the Christian Citadel, what they ultimately accomplished was the fostering of a nascent humanism that would ultimately tear the church asunder. They felt themselves to be the most orthodox of Catholics, and yet every sentence they produced tended to speak for the basic merit and dignity of human faculties as against the quizzical fallibility of theology. Few fit the model of holy heretic more completely than the twelfth century's *enfant terrible*, Peter Abelard (1079–1142).

Abelard is one of those fantastic figures in intellectual history about whom just about anything may be said, and all of it is mostly true. He was an ultra-orthodox hyper-revolutionary. He was a debauched celibate. The most naïve and most cunning of men, Abelard attracted passionate adherents from Europe through the sheer force of his personal improbability.

As the eldest son of a knight, medieval custom seemed to destine him for the martial life, and yet young Peter proved so adept, so quick of wit and insight, in his early schooling that a life of letters called him. Renouncing his right to inherit his father's title and lands, at the age of fourteen he learned at the feet of Roscelin, a brilliant theologian suspected of, and eventually tried for, heresy. Roscelin taught Abelard the ways of logic, and how they might be applied to theological argumentation, and thereby set the young man down a road that would lead from tragedy to tragedy to tragedy.

Pumped up with a youthful sense of his logical infallibility, Abelard made his way to Paris in 1100 and sought out the greatest master of dialectic there to test his strength against. This was William of Champeaux, one of the mighty minds of his time, and not one to suffer insolent students indefinitely. Chased out of Paris by William, Abelard repeated the cycle studying under Anselm of Laon, whom he also routinely insulted and eventually had to flee.

Through all the intellectual sparring, Abelard had made a name for himself as a brilliant logician, and attracted a steady stream of students eager to gain his secrets of disputation. What they learned from him was the duplicity of words, how they changed meaning when used by different people, and how rhetorical tricks might be played in the space between something's substance and its name. Those ideas might seem tiny, but they open up the possibility for a world of doubt when applied to something claiming as absolute a unity in thought as the Catholic Church.

In 1113, William of Champeaux became bishop of Châlons-sur-Marne, and Abelard was able to return to Paris to become a master at Notre Dame. And it was in that capacity that he met Hélöise.

Now, it's easy from our modern, enlightened standpoint to be critical of his behavior with regard to her.

So that's what I'm going to do.

Hélöise's family, however, were outraged by Abelard's behavior subsequent to the wedding (which we saw in all its salacious splendor in the last story). But, to preserve Abelard's budding career, it had to be kept a secret. The two of them decided, without her consent, that he and Hélöise would get married but, to preserve Abelard's budding career, it had to be kept a secret. When some of her family went public with the marriage, she denied it, and Abelard panicked, sending her off to the convent at Argenteuil for safekeeping. Her family thought he was trying to force her to become a nun in order to back out of his marriage, and sent a posse to castrate him. (The procedure, as Abelard described it later, was remarkably painless and sanitary, if you're curious). And so, emasculated and jealous lest she take on another lover, he compelled Hélöise to become a nun against her will, then left her in silence for a decade.

It doesn't look good, even if you take into consideration that Hélöise herself wanted him to do whatever was necessary to preserve his career, regardless of its impact on her life and happiness.

One would think that, after castration and public disgrace, Abelard would have done his level best to keep his head low and coast his way back to respectability. But that is to underestimate Abelard's remarkable sense of self-worth and limitless ego-driven resilience. Finding refuge as a monk at the monastery of St. Denis, he no sooner arrived than he started criticizing his fellow monks for being lax and irreligious. Having thoroughly pissed off everybody there, they sent him off to a place where he could have a few students, continue his teaching, and not get in anybody's way.

At which point he decided to start writing a book of theology which claimed that the pagan philosophers could be just as moral as Christians, and that all religious ideas had to be approached through reason and logic if they were to be truly understood. "By doubting we come to inquiry, and by inquiry we perceive the truth," was his maxim, and a more dangerous idea could hardly have been floated at that time in ecclesiastical history.

The contents of Abelard's new book, *Theologia*, became known, and Abelard was duly commanded to report to the papal legate for judgment. After a mockery of a trial in which Abelard was not allowed to defend his opinions, he was forced to publicly burn his book and read aloud the creed he had supposedly violated through his disturbing notions about how the Trinity might possibly, sort of, be made sensible.

Returning to the monastery of St. Denis again, Abelard did a typical Abelard thing and started making jokes about the doubtful official origin story of the historical St. Denis. This was a grave insult to the monks who already didn't like him much, and to the France which considered the St. Denis monastery as its pure beating heart. Soooooo, Abelard was kicked out, again, and told to be a hermit for a while. Which he did, summoning his students to him in the wilderness while he set to work rewriting his *Theologia* (he had, of course, had a secret spare copy of it so that, in burning the first, he wasn't casting his thoughts to oblivion), as well as a slew of other theological texts of similar rationalistic intent, including *Sic et Non*, his collection of contradictory quotes from church fathers about all of the big questions in Christianity.

Throughout the 1120s and 1130s, he was a man divided among several contradictory goals. He was made abbot of St. Gildas (whose monks he immediately insulted and who, in turn, tried to kill him on more than one occasion), with responsibility for ensuring a steady flow of contributions into its coffers on the strength of the absolute orthodoxy of its monastic practice, while writing works that argued strenuously for a complete re-evaluation of the basic tenets of Christian faith. The legalistic official interpretation of the Redemption, for example, whereby Christ had to be crucified in order to pay off a debt to the devil, Abelard declared to be flatly ridiculous, and replaced it with an explanation based in redemption through love. In fact, for all of his pretense towards complete rationality, the theme of love overcoming dogma appears a number of times in his works, leading to the very verge of the conclusion that, as long as you live a life devoted to the love of your fellow humans, you can't go wrong. Even heavyweight notions like Sin don't apply, so long as your heart and intentions are pure, under Abelard's new system of ethics.

Of course, the Catholic Church could have none of that, and brought Abelard up on charges of heresy again in 1140, this time ordering that all of his books, wheresoever they might be found, be burned, and that Abelard submit to a life of absolute silence until the end of his days. Practically speaking, none of those things ended up happening. The papacy was still recovering from the 1130 split between pope and antipope, and the inquisitional ferocity that would strike terror into Europe in the thirteenth century and beyond was in its bumbling youth in 1140. As it happened, one of Abelard's friends, the influential abbot of Cluny, offered him protection, and the pope accepted the offer as a reasonable solution to everybody's problems.

Abelard was at that time old, and in failing health. He was, though, writing up to the end, preparing yet another edition of the *Theologia* every bit as heretical as the first two, but confident somehow that the next trial would be different. That work remained incomplete, however, as he died in 1142, just two years after his absolute condemnation by Pope Innocent II. Had he lived one more year, he would have seen his good friend installed as Pope Celestine II, and most likely would have, at long last, earned the official recognition he felt due to his boundless genius. As it is, he left behind a legacy of daring rationalism that couldn't help but be dangerous even when it was pressed into the service of justifying orthodox concepts. That same insistence led just as much to the high Scholasticism of Thomas Aquinas as it did to the emerging skepticism of the fifteenth century.

Perhaps more importantly, he was an example of steadfast individualism who couldn't be bound by any single institution or body of thought, and who directly inspired the first organized sallies against Catholic hegemony in the form of his student Arnold of Brescia's democratic, anti-papal Commune of Rome, launched just one year after Abelard's death. And that too-crazy-to-not-be-true event will be the subject of our very next comic, on the very next page!

FURTHER READING:
The source for Abelard is entirely M. T. Clanchy's *Abelard: A Medieval Life*. Yes, it repeats itself all the time (fun drinking game: take a shot every time Clanchy mentions the fact that Guy of Castello never burned his copy of *Sic et Non*) but you won't find any better in terms of a vibrant account of Abelard's pronounced personal faults mixed with a profound respect for his intellectual accomplishments. This is not the romantic Abelard of the nineteenth century, or the intellectually insignificant Abelard of the early twentieth, but precisely Abelard as Abelard, and as a gateway text into the fascinating history of twelfth century thought, one could do worse!

The Archpoet:
Twelfth-Century Gangsta

The twelfth century was an intellectual Wild West. Lying at the very heart of the Dark Ages, it was a time of academic explosion and theological daring that spectacularly collapsed under the weight of its own chutzpah. Popes battled antipopes while kings built empires upon the rubble. Abelard, the greatest mind of his era, was gang-jumped and castrated for having despoiled the virtue of young Héloïse. And amidst all the carnage and jumble, one court poet had a hell of a time getting drunk, writing verse, making money, and calling Rome to account for its hypocrisy. We know him only as The Archpoet.

Yes, that is objectively the coolest name of anybody we're going to be visiting in this series, but beyond that we know precious little about him. His entire fame rests on a mere ten surviving poems, including two featured in that treasury of medieval bawdiness, the *Carmina Burana*. But those ten poems show us a side of the Dark Ages that belies the standard history of Europe.

Let's face it, we like our Dark Ages, well, dark. We want them populated by a shadowy Catholic Church that brooked no dissent, and a people cowed to subservience by the dictates of God and Rome. It's an often true picture of the half millennium separating the fall of Rome from the first stirrings and whirrings of the Renaissance, but by accepting it as comprehensive we lose out on some truly delightful pockets of humanist resistance, such as the wondrous drunken ravings of our new friend The Archpoet.

What we know is that he worked for an archbishop in the service of Frederick Barbarossa, the Holy Roman Emperor whose army criss-crossed Europe in a terribly romantic but overambitious plan to re-establish the Roman Empire with Frederick its ruler, and the pope a merely useful employee of the state. The dates of his life, 1130-1165, are pure educated guesswork based on some contextual clues in the handful of surviving poems we have. For that matter, everything we know about him comes from those poems, so let's dig in.

The most famous is poem X, the "Confession" narrative, but my favorite for sheer nerve is the first. It begins with all the standard moves one would expect of a medieval poet:

Poetarum seductos fabulis
To men seduced by the fables of poets
Veritatis instruxit regulis,
He [Jesus] taught truth and the laws,
Signis multis atque miraculis
By many signs and miracles
Fidem veram dedit incredulis.
He gave true faith to unbelievers.

The usual, right? There follow stanzas upon stanzas in a similar vein, until the Archpoet cunningly turns the topic to Christian charity, and in particular the type of charity owed by a wealthy man, such as the patron to whom the poem is addressed, to a poor man, such as the poet himself. Having greased the wheels of holy charity, he lets loose with his own mock apologetic story:

Vitam meum vobis enucleo,
Let me lay out my life story,
Paupertatem meam non taceo:
and I won't conceal my poverty:
Sic sum pauper et sic indigeo,
So poor am I and in such need,
Quod tam siti quam fame pereo.
That I am quite dying of thirst and hunger.

Non sum nequam, nullum decipio:
But I'm not worthless, nor do I deceive:
Uno tantum laboro vi(c/t)io:
I give injury in only one way:
Nam libenter semper accipio
For I always accept generosity with pleasure
Et plus mihi quam fratri cupio.
And prefer getting more than my brother.

But why does he need such generosity? Well,

Nobis vero mundo fruentibus
For myself, having savored the world's delights
Vinum bonum saepe bibentibus,
And having often drunk good wine
Sine vino deficientibus,
(For without wine I grow weak and useless),
Nummos multos pro largis sumptibus.
Let God grant me much money to wipe out my debts.

Wine, poetry, sex, and sumptuous fur cloaks: as you read through the Archpoet's work, these are the things he sinks his heart into writing about, while the references to religion and to his patron's intelligence and prowess are just so many flattering devices to help get him more wine, sex, and sumptuous fur cloaks. The call to holy obedience can't stand against the call to LIVE, and in spite of his assurances that, with a little more money he'll change his ways and set out on the path of humility, each new poem sees him broke again, and more in love with good wine and good poetry than ever (in poem IV he flat out says that he can outwrite Ovid if he's drunk enough).

Moving from his own love of pleasure and good company to the wider world, the

Archpoet surveys the religious landscape, and rails against the flagrant hypocrisy of the papacy and its priests:

Doleo, cum video leccatores multos
I grieve, when I see the many parasites (priests)
Penitus inutiles penitusque stultos,
Entirely useless and even more stupid,
Nulla prorsus animi ratione fultos
Supported by no ability to reason
Sericis et variis indumentis cultos.
Worshiping in their expensive silk robes.
Pereat hypocrisis omnium parcorum!
Let them perish, these hypocrites who hoard Their wealth!

And the Archpoet wasn't alone in the twelfth century. As we've seen, Abelard's *Sic et Non* was a catalogue of mutually contradictory statements by church fathers. The poetry of Hugh Primas was as critical of the Catholic Church as the Archpoet's. Frederick Barbarossa lent his support to three different antipopes when Pope Alexander III wouldn't submit to his will. In France, the University of Paris was founded mid-century with departments of Medicine, Art, and Law alongside Theology. The pulsing curiosity of the human race was everywhere quickening, spurring intellectuals to think dangerously, kings to act boldly, and poets to live by the dictates of their nature, rather than the abstract precepts of the flagrantly corrupt religious classes.

It didn't last.

When and precisely how our poet died amidst the rush and swell of this mini-Renaissance we can't know. All that remains, then, is to write the epitaph of our blearily heroic poet. Luckily, he wrote his own:

Meum est propositum in taberna mori,
It's a pretty sure bet I'll die in a tavern,
Ut sint vina proxima morientis ori.
And may wine be near my lips upon dying.
Tunc cantabunt letius angelorum chori:
Then will the chorus of angels merrily sing:
"Sit deus propitious huic potatori."
"May God have mercy on this drunkard."

FURTHER READING

You can find all ten of The Archpoet's existing poems online in Latin at **www.thelatin library.com/archpoet.html**.  The most famous of those, poem X, exists in several English translations available on the Internet, but that is not the case for the other nine, which is why all of the translations above are my own. If you can't (or don't wanna) read Latin and you have way more money than I, Fleur Babcock has a collection of the poetry of Hugh Primas and the Archpoet in a dual Latin-English format which is well spoken of.

How Europe Got Its Aristotle Back: The Life and Philosophy of Ibn Rushd (Averroes)

CORDOBA, 1182.

AVERROES!

OH, *YOU*...

I'M SENSING SOME HOSTILITY.

I'M FINE. I MEAN, IT'S NOT LIKE YOU'VE BEEN VISITING RANDOM IGNORANT *PEASANTS** BEFORE FINALLY GETTING AROUND TO *ME*.

* SEE EPISODE 10!

AWWW, DON'T BE LIKE THAT. I'M HERE TO LEARN!

REALLY, ARE YOU SURE YOU DON'T HAVE SOME RAMBLING, SELF-ABSORBED LACKWIT TO VISIT FIRST?

NAW, I DON'T THINK I'M DOING *JUNG* FOR A WHILE YET.

SO, WHAT'S YOUR DEAL?

MY *DEAL* IS THAT I CHANGED THE COURSE OF BOTH ISLAMIC AND WESTERN CIVILIZATION!

MY COMMENTARIES ON ARISTOTLE AND PLATO *REVITALIZED* EUROPEAN THOUGHT AND PROVIDED AN INTELLECTUAL, BROADLY TOLERANT ALTERNATIVE TO ISLAMIC MYSTICISM!

WHOA, THAT'S KINDA RAD.

IT *IS!* YES, IF IT WEREN'T FOR ME, ISLAM WOULDN'T BE THE RATIONAL FORCE FOR REASONABLE SPECULATION YOU *DOUBTLESS* KNOW SO WELL IN YOUR FUTURE!

RIGHT, ABOUT THAT...

In an era when anybody can call up the sum total of human knowledge from any of half a dozen devices within an arm's reach, it's often hard to wrap one's head around the historical fragility of information. And not just via the grand conflagrations—the burning of the Great Library of Alexandria, the closing of the School of Athens—but through that slow, imperceptible vanishing that passes unremarked until what was once the wisdom of a civilization exists only as whispers and rumor, leaving us to wonder how we casually let so much of our cultural past slip through our fingers.

The great example is the West's seven-century-long amnesia as to its classical legacy. From roughly 500 to 1220 CE, Aristotle and Plato lay almost entirely forgotten, the entirety of their formidable knowledge reduced to one translated volume of the former, and a fragment of the latter. The regaining of their intellectual legacy is, among historians of philosophy, almost universally considered the great turning point in Western Civilization, and the man most responsible for it was a Spanish Muslim philosopher who stands as perhaps the only figure in world history to have an equally towering influence in the development of Islamic, Christian, *and* humanist thought.

His name was Ibn Rushd (1126-1198), though we know him as Averroes, or simply *The Commentator*. He came of age during the great flowering of Andalusian thought under the Almohad caliphate. Until that time, Baghdad was the intellectual center of the world, and it was there that the rationalists of the Islamic tradition waged their philosophical war with the traditionalists, armed with the inherited wisdom of the Greeks. In the Western part of the Islamic Empire, however, the traditionalists, those who could not countenance the use of reason in the realm of theology, held sway until the founding of the Almohad Dynasty and its reintroduction of the ancient classics.

Within a half century, Cordoba's intellectual influence was second only to that of Baghdad, and towered over a Parisian academic climate that was just finding its feet. Ibn Rushd was born to a family of celebrated jurists during a time when the rationalist camp had been forced into a corner by the fundamentalist vigor of Al-Ghazali's *Incoherence of the Philosophers*, a work which labeled as heretics all who attempted to philosophically probe the content of Islam. He was the reigning titan of Islamic theology, and in four decades none had stepped forward to contest his vision of strict scriptural obedience.

And then came Ibn Rushd, a man who seemed to master anything he put his mind to. He studied law and medicine, astronomy and philosophy, with some of the greatest minds of Cordoban society, and could have made a full career out of any of them, so easily did proficiency come to him. However, though given the distinguished position of Judge of Seville in 1160, it wasn't until 1169 that he stumbled into his true calling.

The story goes that his friend brought him one day to see Abu Ya'qub Yusuf, the second caliph of the Almohad dynasty. Yusuf asked Ibn Rushd if he believed the sky had existed for all time, or if it had been created at some point. The question seems innocuous and speculative to us, but it was in fact one of the most dangerous things Yusuf could have inquired about. The Muslim community was fiercely split on the issue of the eternity of the world, and the wrong answer could have destroyed Ibn Rushd's career. Quick on his feet, he protested ignorance of the topic, whereupon Yusuf began talking freely of the opinions of the Greeks and other philosophical traditions, putting the rationalist-leaning Ibn Rushd at ease.

The two fell into easy conversation, and Yusuf suggested that Ibn Rushd should write a full set of Aristotelian commentaries. It was an immense task, but that's precisely what Ibn Rushd committed his life to achieving. Displaying a mastery for synthesis, he wrote summaries of all the Aristotelian works then known, and severely criticized the shortcomings of previous Arabic interpretations of The Philosopher. Beyond that, using Aristotle as his firm base, he struck out against the prevailing anti-philosophical bent of Islamic theology, aiming his scorn directly at its most intimidating work, the *Incoherence of the Philosophers*. With a boldness in the face of superior power almost unfathomable today, he wrote a work whose title set the tone for all that was to be found within: *The Incoherence of the Incoherence*.

It was a thorough and merciless attack on Al-Ghazali and everything the fundamentalists had wrongly imputed to the Islamic philosophical movement. Where Al-Ghazali had said, in an attempt to preserve the existence of miracles, that there was no natural order and in fact that God is directly intervening anytime *anything* happens, Ibn Rushd argued that this elaborate attempt to discredit the power of causality was unnecessary, unsound, and admitted of no possible knowledge of the workings of the universe, rendering all science void. Where Al-Ghazali stuck firmly by the Judaeo-Christian-Islamic account of the beginning of the universe, Ibn Rushd declared that all three religions were mistaken in their shared tradition, and that the idea of creation out of nothing was scientifically and philosophically abhorrent. And where the traditionalists maintained steadfastly their exact knowledge of the attributes of God, Ibn Rushd countered with the impossibility of accurately employing nature-derived vocabulary in the description of supernatural capacities.

But the most impressive thing about the book is its pragmatic approach to religion itself. Following Plato's *Republic*, on which he wrote a commentary, Ibn Rushd gives pride of place to philosophy as a way of investigating the world and its truths, and of explaining how a good and happy life is to be achieved, but he recognizes that it is entirely too subtle and intricate for most people to follow. He holds it to be the job of religion, then, to provide laws and enticements to improve the common people's lives. Whichever religion has the best laws at a given time is, by his account, the best religion, and it is to be entirely expected that, no matter how good a religion is now, it will be eventually superseded by something that practically does the job of inspiring the masses better.

On these and many other points, what Ibn Rushd consistently fought for was the right to use reason to illuminate theology and life. It was the responsibility of humans to reach their full intellectual potential by considering the causes of what they saw around them, and with each discovery to climb to higher levels of intellectual clarity. To an Islamic establishment that called for full and unquestioning subservience, and accused of infidelity all who dared question the content of religion, Ibn Rushd responded that the true infidelity was disobeying God's command to investigate reality, to be

given a divine instrument like the brain and then not use it to its fullest.

His works were understandably controversial in Islamic circles, and towards the end of his life, during a moment when the caliphate needed to appease the orthodox elements of the empire, he was sent into exile and his books burned, though he was called back once the political situation had cooled. Roundly condemned by most, his influence as the greatest expositor of Islamic rationalism nevertheless survived as a strand of Islamic thought down to the present day, a constant reminder of Another Way for those oppressed by the strictures of Islamic belief.

That he was a massive figure in the history of Islamic thought (and I haven't even touched upon his definitive contribution to Islamic jurisprudence) there is no doubt. But for those of us in the West, his contribution to our intellectual life is if anything *more* pronounced than his domestic legacy. His works were taken up with an unabashed zeal by the Spanish Jewish community, and translated with an astonishing rapidity by a culture that found in his treatment of Aristotle and Plato a whole new world of intellectual possibility. From Spain, his works passed to Europe via the translations of Michael the Scot, William de Luna, and everybody's favorite medieval translator, Hermann the German. (You just snickered, didn't you? So immature.)

To a Europe that had known only a book and change of the entire Platonic-Aristotelian tradition, the arrival of Ibn Rushd's complete commentaries on all known works of Aristotle was a thunderbolt. While Aristotle came to be known by medieval scholars as *The Philosopher*, Ibn Rushd became simply *The Commentator*.

He was a hero to Siger of Brabant and Boetius of Dacia and, even when arguing against him, the influence of Ibn Rushd is very much present in the Aristotelianism of Thomas Aquinas. Aristotle's teleological approach to investigating the cosmos became, as a result of Ibn Rushd's masterful expositions, the dominant intellectual force for the next four centuries of European thought.

More than that, he has often been credited as well with the founding of modern skeptical philosophy, centuries before Descartes. His rational approach to theology inspired the Averroist movement, which was eventually condemned by the church as being tantamount to atheism, and which served as the source for luminaries like Dante Alighieri in arguing for the separation of church and state, and other philosophers to argue that if investigation and reason deemed something to be true, then religious tradition *had* to give way. Regardless of whether Ibn Rushd would have condoned the conclusions that people derived from his work, the fact that his thought was so rich as to inspire internal changes to Islam and Christianity, as well as providing the raw material for a philosophical school a good four hundred years ahead of its time, speaks to the breadth of his philosophical project.

Now, there's one of you out there who has been very patient while dying to ask a question. Now is your chance.

"But isn't Aristotelianism *bad*? Didn't scientific progress come to a dead stop until we broke away from teleological explanations of nature? Why are we celebrating this dude, then, for bringing us a set of works that delayed for centuries our intellectual progress?"

That's a very fair question. If Plato was the Bad Greek of late nineteenth century phi-

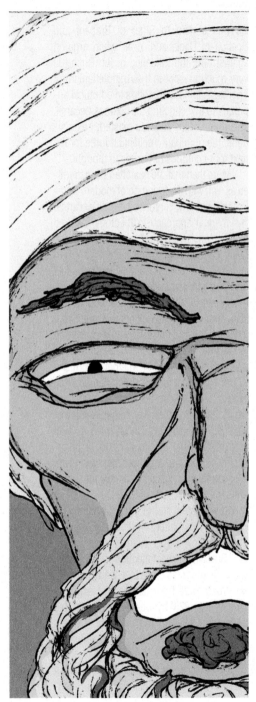

losophy, Aristotle was that of the twentieth, as historians of science pieced together what made our scientific revolution possible and came to the conclusion that it was when Aristotelian *why*-type explanations were replaced by Newtonian *how*-type ones. And that's a very important observation, but let's not forget what Aristotle improved upon. Faced with the Platonic conception of a world of Forms that exist outside of their physical instantiations, Aristotle called foul and said that the way we know things is by abstracting from the real. Intellectual inquiry for Aristotle is not a matter of positing metaphysical absolutes behind mere reality, but is rather an investigation of how things came to be the way they are.

That was a hugely important adjustment to make—it put the focus back on the world as it is, and if his successors became so wrapped up in the potential of this cause-and-goal way of looking at the world, to the point that it took them centuries to do for Aristotelian thought what he had done to Platonic belief, it's because of the raw power of his notion of causality. It

got people thinking about mechanisms of change and motion, and that was all for the ultimate good. Had it been Plato's works, and not those of Aristotle, that Ibn Rushd concentrated on explaining, the Scientific Revolution would likely have taken even longer, and had he not existed, leaving the more modest accountings of Avicenna and other Arabic commentators to do their work, the delay would have been longer still.

All roads lead from Ibn Rushd. In him, the three great religious traditions of the West met with a full accounting of the wisdom of antiquity and found a synthesis that would define the Western intellectual project for centuries to come, and a tension that would set the stage for the great rationalist turn that we are still enjoying. In the near millennium since his death, the only figure of remotely comparable stature in terms of philosophical impact on the structure of world thought is Karl Marx, and yet a stroll down Berkeley's Telegraph Avenue will net one very few Ibn Rushd-inspired tee-shirts. He's the world historical intellectual figure we've decided to forget about. And that's rather too bad.

FURTHER READING

If you don't read Arabic, your options are pretty limited in terms of works concentrating solely on Ibn Rushd. I think Majid Fakhry's *Averroes: His Life, Works, and Influence* is a nice, brief introduction that highlights the revolutionary aspects of Ibn Rushd's thought without overlooking the areas in which he was more of a compiler than an innovator. If you read French, the godfather of Western sources for Averroes is the great Ernest Renan's 1852 *Averroes et l'Averoissme*, which is pretty easy to flag down in print-on-demand form. The works of Averroes were made available in Latin in the '60s in an eleven volume edition, but for English your starting point is probably the Simon van den Bergh translation of *Incoherence*.

A Monk of Nature: The Medieval Science of Albertus Magnus

COLOGNE, 1252.

ALBERT! HEY HEY HEY!

SH! I HAVE BEEN OBSERVING THIS CREATURE FOR DAYS NOW, TRYING TO EMPIRICALLY SETTLE A MATTER OF BIOLOGICAL FACT.

ABOUT THAT OSTRICH?

YES, SEVERAL REPUTABLE AUTHORS HAVE SAID THAT IT HATCHES ITS EGGS BY LOOKING AT THEM.

EGG HATCHING EYE BEAMS? DAMN I'LL MISS THE MIDDLE AGES. SO, YOU'RE WRITING YOUR OBSERVATIONS?

NO, I'M *REMEMBERING* MY OBSERVATIONS. I'M *WRITING* A CHAPTER ON ARISTOTLE'S TELEOLOGICAL CONCEPTION OF INTELLECT...

SURE. AND WITH YOUR *LEFT* HAND?

MERELY RESTRUCTURING THE FINANCIAL OPERATUS OF THE REGENSBURG BISHOPRIC. ONE MUST KEEP ON TOP OF THESE THINGS!

LIKE WHEN YOU WANT TO TWEET A SELFIE OF YOURSELF WITH A MOUSTACHE NECKLACE, BUT THEN ALSO WANT TO FACE TIME WITH YOUR FRIENDS TO TALK ABOUT *WANTING* TO TWEET THE SELFIE?

THAT SOUNDS BOTH EXHAUSTING AND VACUOUS.

YUP! IT'S GREAT!

Albertus Magnus was one of those individuals seemingly born for the sole purpose of making the rest of humanity feel insignificant and under-achieving. By every possible metric, he stuffed ten lifetimes of work, research, writing, and thought into his eight decades. He was a master in whatever field he touched with his intellect, a voracious devourer of ideas and experience, and wherever his interest was drawn, something revolutionary was bound to happen.

Of his early life, we know frustratingly little. He was either born in 1193 or 1206, depending on the historian you ask, though all agree he was probably of minor Swabian nobility. After that, we have nothing but rumor and improbable legend until he joined the order of the Dominicans in either 1223 or 1229. For those first three decades, all we have are glimpses provided by Albert himself, of a boy scrambling through the German countryside, investigating nature, and being drawn to the intellectual and mystical puzzles of Christianity.

He was, above all things, a collector and synthesizer of facts and ideas. He believed fervently that everything was connected to everything else, and that one man's well-considered truths did not become in-validated just because that man was Jewish, Muslim, or pagan. He devoured the Arabic commentaries of Avicenna and Averroes on Aristotle's works, and saw in the Greek's grand vision a new path for Western science, philosophy, and theology.

It was not, however, a path to be blindly followed. Unlike many Aristotelian natural philosophers of the next three centuries, Albert was a profound believer in Finding Things Out For Yourself. Of the estimated 138 books he wrote, his most renowned are those recording his

observations in botany and taxonomy. Centuries before Linnaeus, he was possessed of a need to systematize the startling diversity of life on this planet. He searched for common traits, performing painstaking dissections of insects and plants, fish and fowl, to discover the micro-structures that link related animals together. His deftness with the scalpel allowed him to find differentiated sub-layers where previous scientists had only found contiguous matter, to follow the nerves of flies, and repudiate the most firmly held beliefs of a millennium of biological wisdom.

It's for this latter service that we have the greatest reason to keep Albertus Magnus in our collective memory. Confronted with a medievalism that believed firmly in the biological wisdom of the mystical creature bestrewn *Physiologus*, Albert went out into the forests and plains and found the animals spoken of, watched their habits, their birth and life and death, and investigated their anatomical structures. Whenever he found the mighty Aristotle in error, he raised the cry that new observations must trump old writings.

When Albert couldn't determine directly the truth of a statement, he sought out those who had personal experience with the animals, minerals, and plants written of in the ancient sources—falcon keepers and metal workers, quarry managers and foresters. His travels on Dominican business took him all over Europe, and everywhere he went he sought out examples of local flora and fauna and mined the expertise of the region's craftsmen and farmers. In this way, he was able to definitively eliminate much of the purely superstitious content of Aristotelian and medieval natural wisdom, and more importantly to establish a creed that old beliefs require constant new evaluation, an idea that

would have worked much good had it not taken three centuries to catch on.

Not content with having merely mapped a path for botany, physics, mineralogy, comparative anatomy, taxonomy, and astronomy to follow, Albert was also the greatest philosophical systematizer of his day, the teacher of Thomas Aquinas and life source for a broad and intense Scholasticism of so penetrating an intent that it ended by ripping its own foundations apart. He came of academic age during the great wave of Jewish and Arabic scholarship that gave the West its first stunning glimpses of the full breadth of Aristotelian and Platonic thought. While some fought vigorously against the foreign onslaught, Albert embraced it, seeking out everywhere new ideas that he could weld to the philosophically anemic body of Christian thought to create, at last, an intellectually rigorous Christian theology.

Up to then, the best philosophical under-pinnings that Christianity could muster were the Neoplatonic musings of St. Augustine, the logical pyrotechnics of Peter Abelard, and the obscure mysticism of pseudo-Dionysius. Neoplatonism was interesting, but failed utterly at resolving many of the most glaring contradictions at the heart of Christianity. Abelard's project, all self-pitying claims to the contrary, was mostly destructive in its results. And nobody really quite knew just what pseuo-Dionysius was on about, other than that it was terribly mysterious. Something rigorous needed to be done.

The job would require somebody of exquisite breadth of learning and an intense capacity for systematization. Albert, and more famously his student Thomas Aquinas, managed the task by implanting an Aristotelian backbone in the body of Christian belief, providing a worked-out and profound structure onto which Christianity's more diffuse notions could be plausibly hung. Aristotelian teleology, with its rigid sense of hierarchy and purpose, replaced the more poetic notions of Plato, to affect a conception of God, the creation of the universe, and man, which held together better than anything of the previous millennium and a half.

More significantly, the application of Jewish, Arabic, Greek, and mystic ideas to philosophically prop up the body of Catholic thought made Albert's theology a far more cosmopolitan enterprise than anything attempted previously, a multi-denominational struggle after the meaning of the universe that didn't care where answers came from so long as they were rational and consistent. Albert himself was too caught up emotionally in his life as a Dominican to take that idea to its fullest conclusion—that would have to wait for Descartes and eventually the Enlightenment. But the intellectual ideal that he constructed survived within Catholic thought and drove a counter-community of Catholics to the sciences and a broadly tolerant view of other cultures. Overshadowed by the Inquisitions and heresy-hunters of the pre-Reformation era, these scientifically leaning intellectuals are just now being rediscovered and appreciated for their paradoxical role in advancing natural philosophy.

What makes Albert's intellectual achievement all the more remarkable is that writing was not the primary thing that he did—it was what he did on his off-hours. Most of the time, he was traveling across Europe, undertaking commissions from both the master of his order and the pope. Well into his eighties, he was running these religious errands, giving dispensations for religious festivals to offer forty-day indulgences to all attendees (the grandfather of the First 500 Fans Get a Free Bobblehead ploy), hearing disputes between the secular and religious leadership, whipping up support for a new crusade in Germany, establishing new monkeries, and even taking on a two-year stint as a bishop.

His time and reputation were constantly under the demands of others, but he made his own opportunities for observation. When food was brought to him at the table, while his fellow monks shoveled the teeming courses into their maws, he would first investigate what was before him—what type of fish was this, what was its skeletal structure? How would one describe the pigment of this fruit, how best to dissect the sensations of its taste? Each moment was a learning experience, filed away in his immaculate memory for inclusion in a book later.

He was a Catholic, absolutely—believed in God and the Trinity, had a getting-towards-creepy obsession with the Virgin Mary, and shot through reams of parchment trying to create a consistent system from the content of Christianity's mystical traditions. So, why include him in a history of humanism? Certainly, his books on botany and animal classification stand as the greatest and most empirically driven scientific work of the Middle Ages (though we need to give an honorable mention to Frederick II's *De Arte Venandi cum Avibus* for also being a pretty kick-ass medieval collection of natural experiments). Really, that ought to be enough to earn the affection of anybody with the slightest secular leaning. But far more than that, we should recognize the humanism of his spirit—the acceptance of great minds from all cultures, the striving for synthesis and consistency, and the omnipresent curiosity about this world in all of its irrepressible variety. These are all qualities that any humanist today would be proud to possess. They all existed in one medieval man, in spite of a culture that tended to brand curiosity as heresy and inclusivity likewise, is astounding.

Yes, what we think of as the start of the Humanist Era of our history did not take place until centuries after Albertus Magnus, and its birth can be pinpointed to the moment when his monumental philosophical system was at last torn down. But the tools used in that destruction were ones that Albert himself crafted—the reluctance to accept authority, the need to evaluate for one's self the truth of an assertion, and the use of the best ideas at hand. Had you asked Albert why he wrote those hundred plus books, he would have answered unhesitatingly, "For the greater glory of God." But in practice his curious spirit was simply too broad, too voraciously all-consuming, to remain tethered to anything as small as a god. It was a mind that will have something to offer all of us so long as we wander through nature, and wonder at what we find.

FURTHER READING

There's something wrong with just about every Albertus Magnus book out there. In English, your best choice is probably the old English translation of Hieronymus Wilms's biography (1930). It is comically sycophantic, and its position on This New Fangled Evolution Thing is so wrong as to be almost beautiful, but the first half of the book is a legitimately useful guide for Albert's significance in natural science and religious philosophy.

(Peasant) Girls Just Wanna Have Fun: The Heresy of Grazida Lizier

Heresy-wise, it's hard to beat the early thirteenth century. In northern Italy, southern France, and throughout Germany, thousands of individuals rose, as much disgusted by the church's excesses as inspired by its attempt at self-reform, and crafted local theologies that were part-ancient tradition, part-Christianity, and entirely revolutionary. For a century, the Cathars and Waldensians, Passagians and Arnoldists organized a threat to Catholicism so great in appearance (if not in fact) that the church saw no way out but to let loose the Dominicans and the dread force of Inquisition.

In the midst of this battle for scriptural orthodoxy were the common people, hungry for a way out of the spiritual impasse of worldly Catholicism. Lone humans, making what sense they could of the conflicting authority around them, often guided more by their innate moral instincts than by a fundamental need to preserve some dogmatic core of belief. None speak more eloquently to this trend than Grazida Lizier, a commoner from the South of France whose entire record of existence consists of a few scant pages of testimony taken down by Cathar-hunter extraordinaire Jacques Fournier in 1320. In those lines, a humble mind sets forth what she understood of the universe and its workings, and in a few devastating lines unmakes the cocksure dominance of Catholic orthodoxy.

But to understand why she was being questioned in the first place, we have to talk about Cathars. Which is just as well, because they are lusciously fascinating. They were dualists, which is to say that, faced with the problem of the overwhelming evil present in a world constructed by a supposedly good God, they split the cosmos in two, declaring that everything material was actually constructed by Satan, who peopled his world by imprisoning the souls of God's angels in flesh, while God dwelt in an ethereal, entirely Other realm.

Now, the Old Testament is *rather* clear about Jehovah making the physical Earth, which meant that Cathars variously believed that (1) the Old Testament ought to be thrown out entirely, or (2) that it is correct, but that the Jehovah of that book was actually Satan.

Personally, I think that option two explains *a lot* about the Old Testament's often horrendous moral sense, but the Catholic Church understandably didn't see it that way, nor did it particularly like the Cathar claim that Jesus could not possibly have been a real man, but rather was an essence made to appear as a man. Their new spin on an old problem, combined with their vows of complete austerity (it was common Cathar practice to, after receiving their final baptism, starve themselves to death to avoid pollution of the things of the world) made the movement wildly popular in both southern France and the Italian realms still under the influence of Arnold of Brescia's revolution against church authority.

The problem was that the church didn't really have a firm grasp on what heresy was, or how it was to be dealt with when the Cathars and Waldensians started flowering in the late twelfth century. There wasn't a standardized set of questions to ask, or a routine procedure to follow when trying to determine if a thought was heretical or merely eccentric. Catholicism was caught thoroughly flat-footed as the Cathars and other heretical sects lurched past them in the hearts and minds of a Europe growing weary of the pope's fumbling half-measures towards basic decency.

Jacques Fournier, who would go on to become Pope Benedict XII, was a man determined to bring order to the hunt for heresy, and wandered through southern France, interrogating the Cathars that his ring of informants ratted out to him.

In 1320 he met Grazida Lizier, a peasant from Montaillou, questioned her, incarcerated her for two months, and then questioned her again. This was all of a piece with the rest of Grazida's storm-tossed life. She was born around 1298, and at age fourteen her virginity was taken by the local rector, Pierre Clergue, with the full knowledge of her mother. He continued using her for sex until marrying her, at the age of fifteen, to a pliable man who looked the other way whenever Clergue came to sexually appropriate his wife. Grazida's husband threw her out of the house when she was nineteen, not because of her adultery, but because she wouldn't join his religious sect. So, she was forced to make a living as a barkeep, at least until age twenty-one when she was arrested by Fournier as an adulteress and possible heretic.

Clergue was a Cathar, and in between sexual encounters, he imparted to Grazida some of the tenets of his religion. But then Grazida did something altogether remarkable for a young adult in any age—she held up each of those Cathar beliefs, weighed them against her own internal moral compass, and crafted a new, wholly individual accounting of how the universe worked. It's worth quoting at some length from the original inquisitorial document:

Asked if she believed whether a man sins who has sex with a woman not related to him by blood, a virgin or not, in marriage or out of it, only because it is pleasing to both, she responded that, although all carnal unions of men and women are displeasing to God, however she did not believe that those performing such acts—so long as both derived pleasure from them—commit a sin.

Asked if she believed that those who act well and live sanctified lives go to Paradise after death, while sinners enter Hell, and if she believed there to be a Paradise and Hell, she responded that she didn't know, but she heard it said, that there is a Paradise, and she believes it; she also heard that there is a Hell, but this, she said, she neither believed nor disbelieved...since it is an evil place. Asked in the same manner about resurrection, she said she neither believed nor disbelieved, although she frequently heard it said that we shall rise again.

Let's stop for a moment to appreciate the inventive boldness of Grazida here. On one hand were the Catholics, insisting absolutely in the existence of heaven, hell, resurrection, and the sinfulness of sex outside of marriage. On the other are the Cathars, dismally opposed to all sexual unions, Hell, resurrection, and anything of the earth. And in between those massive boulders of absolutist dogma is this peasant girl who asserts, in the very face of a Catholic inquisitioner, that sex is sex, and though it might displease God, it's certainly no sin as long as everybody is enjoying themselves, that heaven is probably real, but hell is kinda shaky, as she can't conceive of why a good God would have made such an evil place, and that our bodily resurrection seems like a longshot as well.

And, while Grazida's testimony is among the most frank in its assessment of current theology, it is by no means unique. Fournier's records include accounts of women who believe in the general salvation of all men, those who completely deny any afterlife at all, and those who experienced moments of total disbelief in God himself. Indeed, Fournier's reports were on the tail end of a troubling wave of information, starting from the early thirteenth century, documenting a surge of heretical sects throughout France, Italy, and Eastern Europe. Something needed to be done, some organization empowered to draw up regulations for the identification and prosecution of heresy.

In 1252, the pope had granted the Dominicans the right to use torture in weeding out heresy and after that it was off to the races. With the help of obliging monarchs in France, Aragon, and Germany, and the creation of standard inquisitorial processes, the Cathars and Waldensians were driven underground such that, by 1320, when Grazida was being held for questioning by Fournier, the movements were shattered husks of their former selves.

And yet, in spite of the organization of the Inquisition, the viciousness of its techniques, and the alliance between Rome and monarch in the prosecution of heretics, the strands of heterodox doubt were still vibrant enough to produce Grazida Lizier, and a host of others like her. As a brave rebel princess once remarked to an imperial administrator, "The more you tighten your grip, the more star systems slip through your fingers."

Though the Cathars couldn't organize effectively any longer, the circumstances that created the Cathar heresy were still very much present and indeed worsening thanks to the torture-licious exuberance of the Dominicans. The worse a place they made the world to live in, the more plausible did Dualistic theology become, and the stronger Dualism became, the more doubt there was about the validity of theological posturing generally. Grazida was created in that space between orthodoxy and its combatants, a bold testament to how the lunge towards hegemony leaves a million scrambling microscopic heterodoxies in its wake, if you take the time to look.

FURTHER READING

The translation of Grazida's testimony above is my own. The original Latin text (along with that of several other women collected by Fournier) is available in the appendix of Peter Dronke's wonderful *Women Writers of the Middle Ages*. For those interested in medieval heresy, a great sourcebook is Walter Wakefield and Austin Evans's *Heresies of the High Middle Ages*, which contains 640 pages of original documents in English translation relating to the Cathars, Waldensians, and everybody in between. There is also a novel about Grazida and the persecution of the Cathars, *The Good Men*, by Charmaine Craig, which I admit to owning but never having read. Cover's nice, though.

Giovanni Boccaccio: Master of Mythology and Softcore Fourteenth-Century Erotica

NAPLES, 1362.

HEY BOCCACCIO!

YOU, YOU SEEM TO BE FROM THE FUTURE. YOU SEE FROM THIS RATTY BED AND DISMAL ROOM HOW EVEN MY FRIENDS TREAT ME NOW.

TELL ME, IN THE FUTURE, ARE MY WORKS REMEMBERED?

OH, ABSOLUTELY!

REALLY?! DO YOU KNOW ME, THEN, AS A MYTHOLOGIST? THE MAN WHO SCOURED EUROPE FOR ANCIENT MANUSCRIPTS AND THEN PRESERVED THEM IN MY WRITINGS?!

NOT – EXACTLY....

THEN PERHAPS AS THE MAN WHO MADE LEONTIUS COMPLETE HIS TRANSLATION OF THE ILIAD, RENDERING IT AVAILABLE TO THE WORLD?

THAT WAS YOU? *NEAT*, THANKS MAN.

APPARENTLY NOT.

PERHAPS FOR REVITALIZING VERNACULAR POETRY?

NOT QUITE, NO.

SIGH IT'S THE SEX BOOKS, ISN'T IT?

TOTALLY! SOME EDITIONS IN MY DAY EVEN COME PACKED WITH FEATHERS AND EROTIC OILS!

For six hundred years, before, "Did somebody here call a plumber?" and, "Did somebody here call a second, hunkier plumber?" the lifeblood of Western erotica was drawn from a series of stories improbably written during the depths of the Black Plague. As two out of three Florentines died in the course of a single year, one man wrote a book that formed the basis not only of Europe's erotic imagination, but the foundation of narrative fiction itself, for the next half-millennium. That book was the *Decameron*, and the rotund mass of excitable contradictions that penned it stands at the very threshold of modern humanist fiction.

Giovanni Boccaccio (1313-1375) was, like Leonardo da Vinci, an illegitimate child. Unlike Leonardo, however, his father was quick to bring him into his new family and business, entrusting him with the most important of tasks, and generally making illegitimacy seem so light a burden that Boccaccio passed the favor forward by siring five illegitimate children of his own later.

His father was a businessman invested deeply in fostering economic relations between Florence and Naples, and it was the vivacious world of the marketplace that stamped Boccaccio's early life. While the clerics and academics scribbled away in towers, agonizing over the twists and turns of Scholasticism, Boccaccio was doing business with traders from all parts of the world, grappling with the unique humanity of each, and the many ways by which people seek purpose and pleasure. His early books, including the *Decameron*, were celebrations of this hectic merchant-class spirit, of love and duplicity, compassion and lust, all jostling against each other to produce People, As They Are.

With that background, Boccaccio could have led a thoroughly robust, eminently enjoyable, and entirely forgotten life as one of the thousands of merchants working their way valiantly, if not always quite honestly, to the heart of the post-feudal world. But it so happened that he also was allowed to pursue an entirely unique course of education as well. While he was supposed to be studying law, he was actually learning at the feet of some of the most eclectic minds of fourteenth-century Italy. Their interest was in learning Everything, in gathering all of human knowledge up and using it to create works of imposing referential erudition but little psychological insight. Under their spell, Boccaccio wrote his early works, imitations of his favorite authors spattered with references to antiquity and given to explosive bouts of whimsical autobiographical ecstasy and bottomless grief. In the *Filocolo* (1336), he veers wildly between styles, a *tour de force* pastiche of everything available in the literary air at the time, driven forward by his unrestrained emotionalism.

He was trying everything that literary life had to offer, digesting it, and reproducing it at first as a gifted mimic, and ultimately fusing the voices of a continent together into the narrative pulse that would drive Europe away from the grandeur of the epic, towards the psychological complexity of the domestic and mercantile spheres. He mixed the elegance of the Latin classics with the simple emotionality of French balladry, and at the end of the day, he had forged the modern secular Storytelling Voice, which would inspire Chaucer some decades later to summon English literature forth from the ether.

In 1341 and 1342, returning to Florence after his formative years at Naples, he wrote the *Comedia delle Ninfe* and the *Amorosa Visione*, which accelerated the turn towards the middle class as the subject of fiction, and of the qualities and needs of the heart as superior to all other concerns. He was finding his voice, but it was still hemmed in by the need to Dazzle With Erudition. He wanted to put all that he knew on the page, while at the same time staying true to a realistic portrayal of humanity and its foibles, a tension that was only decided in favor of reality at last when that reality came barreling grimly down upon him and everyone he loved.

For 1348 was a plague year. For Florence, it was *the* plague year. When it ended, only one out of every three citizens remained. In the midst of omnipresent death, half the survivors threw themselves into religious extremism, while the others lost themselves in chasing pleasure while they could, ripping to tatters the web of traditional wisdom that had driven society automatically on, and making room for something new. It is that sense of reworking the boundaries of humanity's potential in the midst of absolute tragedy that gives the *Decameron* a fearless radiance that excites still.

That, and all the sex.

Because, let's face it, the *Decameron* is as much a masterpiece of new narrative style as it is a shameless erotic smorgasbord. The entire third chapter is composed almost exclusively of stories that center around elaborate schemes that culminate in serial humping. A convent gardener is used as an object of sexual pleasure by every nun on the premises until he gets too worn out to work and pleads for a more sensible love schedule. An abbot tricks a man into believing he is dead, and keeps him in a dark room, convincing him it is purgatory, to cure the man of his jealousy, all while flagrantly carrying on a hot affair with his wife.

Two lovers use a monk as their unwitting go-between to pass messages about likely times to meet for mutual carnal knowledge. A woman gets fed up with her husband, who will only have sex on days that aren't religious holidays, and runs off with a pirate king to make mad unrestrained love multiple times a day. A woman cheats on her husband in the husband's full view and somehow manages to convince him that it was a vision induced by a magic pear tree.

A holy hermit, overcome by the beauty of a visitor, convinces her that his penis is the devil, and her vagina is hell, and that, as good Christians, they must find a way to put the devil back in Hell, mustn't they?

The heroes are cunning tricksters, impelled by love or something slightly less pure to twist the social system to their advantage. One of the earliest stories features a greedy and utterly profane merchant who, by dint of a cunning and entirely insincere

deathbed confession, manages not only to get his hosts out of a sticky situation, but also to get himself canonized in the process! Rapscallions become saints. Saints become horny lechers like the rest of us. And the most consistent heroes are not brave Christian knights, but honorable Muslim rulers, impassioned lovers, and poor but clever scamps of every flavor.

It's a Great Book that also happens to be a great book. In those one hundred stories lies the seed of everything we consider now to be a good yarn. The scoundrels whom you can't help but root for, the teenagers risking everything to outwit the system in order to enjoy a perfect day, the women who are frank about their desires and rather fed up with being treated as incorruptible marble objects. Han Solo. Ferris Bueller. Carrie Bradshaw. Boccaccio gave us leave to care seriously about characters like these and their stories, and we haven't stopped caring since.

After the plague, Boccaccio was absorbed equally in tasks diplomatic and literary. His status as the great writer of Florence meant that, whenever a diplomatic mission needed that extra savor of distinction, he was put in charge of it and packed off to some corner of Italy for a while. That might have given him yet more material for a second *Decameron*, but he was decisively rerouted to other pursuits by the advice and friendship of the man he looked up to as the greatest poet and mind of his age, Petrarch.

Petrarch was the great influence in the second half of Boccaccio's life, and it's hard to say whether that was for good or for ill. The two shared a beautifully nerdy love of the works of antiquity, bubbling over with glee whenever one or the other unearthed a rare Latin manuscript in their travels.

Together, they pushed Leontius Pilatus to translate Homer's works into Latin and so to add another shade altogether to European literary life. (Incidentally, after a troubled life, Leontius died when struck by lightning, a rather fitting end, when you think about it.) Petrarch encouraged Boccaccio to continue work on the great compilations of Boccaccio's later life, including the massive and authoritative collection of ancient mythology, the *Genealogica*, which reigned for centuries as the standard text on the study of mythology and contained a stirring defense of the study of pagan beliefs. He also buttressed Boccaccio's belief in the project of vernacular poetry, and together their amassed prestige pushed poetry into a place of prominence in Western intellectual life. And, on the human side, he was a friend, somebody who understood the younger man's bursts of temper, and who always had a room available whenever fortune took a downturn, which it often did.

However.

He was also a Christian moralist who drove Boccaccio to a life of contemplative solitude, to ponderous moral reflection, and to an increasing cynicism about the world and the pleasure to be had in it. The boy who ran through the marketplace and university, absorbing everything he heard and turning it into a new sense of narrative promise had become the scholarly hermit, obsessing over politics and whether the last letter he wrote to Petrarch had been quite flattering enough. From having written a startling collection of the lives of famous women, he fell to authoring a nasty and misogynist rant, the *Corbaccio* (1365). He felt ashamed of the impulses that had made him such an intoxicating writer, and

retreated as an independent artist. He was looking backwards, to Dante and the works of Rome and Greece, and sideways, to Petrarch, but no longer forward.

Not that he needed to. The *Decameron* was such a complete Europe-wide success that he could have rested on its merits the rest of his career. Instead, he produced a definitive accounting of ancient mythology, saved countless precious manuscripts from destruction, brought us the *Iliad* and the *Odyssey*, wrote the first work devoted exclusively to giving full credit to woman's place in history, and played an important role in organizing a new generation of writers to create poetry and narratives in their

country's native tongue about the everyday people they knew. He found a new self which, if less sexy than Boccaccio Mark 1, was as useful in the grand project of collecting and appreciating the vastness of human belief.

In 1374, Petrarch died, and bequeathed to his friend Boccaccio his fur mantle, knowing how bitterly the cold of his often poor lodgings bit at the younger poet's bones. One year later, Boccaccio passed away while wrapped in that very mantle, and if the case can be made that the real Boccaccio died twenty years earlier, suffocated by the overbearing moral mantle of Petrarch, at least both kept him warm.

FURTHER READING

The *Decameron* can be found anywhere. It is one of those books you need to have on hand at all times in order to be called a bookshop. *On Famous Women,* his collection of a hundred plus biographies of famous women, is also readily available in English translation. *Amorosa Visione* was finally translated into English for the first time in 1986, and will run you about $100 for a used copy, so best of luck with that. A first volume of Boccaccio's massive *Genealogica* was finally released in English in 2011, and runs to a modest 928 pages if you want to get *really* into the roots of European mythological studies. For biographies of Boccaccio, Branca's 1976 *Boccaccio: The Man and his Works* gives you a good sense of Boccaccio's literary importance, though if you don't know Latin, the extensive untranslated quotes might be a bit bothersome.

Failing on the Side of Greatness: The Life and Thought of Leonardo da Vinci

Leonardo? Psh. Overrated.

Among humanity's Not Ever Thought sentences, this must rank as one of the NotEverThoughtest. Nearly five hundred years after his death, Leonardo da Vinci (1452-1519) is still humanity's human, our great example, held up to the universe, to justify our existence as a species: "We made this man once, let us persist, and we may make another." He is the "universal man" whose grand failures (and there were many) render him, if anything, a more stunning figure than his celebrated successes.

And he was a bastard. Born out of wedlock to a rising-star notary in 1452, he was packed quietly away to live with his grandparents, far from his father's legitimate family and the eyes of rumor-hungry Florentine society. Leonardo never stopped feeling the sting of his awkward social position, or the loneliness of having been abandoned. His notebooks pulse painfully with allegories expressing the agony of parental neglect, all the more raw for being so desperately hidden in the language of self-distancing mythology.

As an illegitimate son, he received no formal education, a deficit he would scramble to correct in later life, and instead spent a rural youth engaging with the wonders of the countryside. One of the most beautiful things about him was the fact that his childhood sensitivity to the beauty of life in all of its forms did not leave him upon entry into the practical world of adult things. He was a vegetarian out of fondness for animals, bought caged birds at the marketplace just to set them free, and would get angry if he heard people boasting of their hunting exploits. That all life, and not just that of humans, is worthy of respect and protection, is something he brought to the European consciousness, and would merit him a place on a list of humanism's benefactors on its own.

Of course, there is slightly more to Leonardo than an advanced perspective on our connection with the animals. Leonardo's gift for drawing manifested itself early, and his father, recognizing a solution to his problem of What to Do With Leo, signed him on at about the age of fourteen as an apprentice to the Florentine artist-of-all-trades Verrocchio.

It takes a bit of imagining to conjure the world that Leonardo then found himself in. The idea of the lone artist, struggling to perfect his masterpiece while shutting out the world, was so successfully dispersed in the nineteenth century that it overwrote our conception of how artists have historically lived and worked. We think of Leonardo or Botticelli as tortured geniuses slaving over their great canvases, and forget that, most of the time, they were designing disposable amusements for the wealthy, engineering special effects for public celebrations, or painting clock faces for the local convent. An artist's studio in the fifteenth century did anything and everything asked of it. Verrocchio was just as happy to design costumes for a wicked awesome de Medici party as to craft and place the grand globe sitting atop Brunelleschi's dome. Serious commissions and frivolities jostled against each other for workshop space, and an artist was expected to be master of all of these.

This was Leonardo's environment for a decade, as he learned the new techniques in oil painting brought from the north while taking copious notes on casting bronze and producing the pyrotechnic illusions all the rage with the nobility. It was, if anything, a better education than that received by the legitimate children of the middle class. In place of Latin and theology, he learned chemistry and engineering, art and mythology, bookkeeping and politics. A person with a mind hungry for knowledge had a world of it available for consumption at Verrocchio's workshop, and it is our good fortune that he ended up there and not in the hands of a string of bourgeois tutors drilling him on *puella, puellae, puellam*…

Leonardo the Artist bloomed in this atmosphere and came to his full flowering in Milan, but it is Leonardo the Thinker we're going to focus on. Towards the end of his career, he repeatedly claimed to be painting-weary, and only produced new works under patronal duress, but he never stopped learning and inventing. When left to his own devices, he actively sought engineering work, or artistic work that had a clear engineering challenge to it, such as the giant bronze horse of Milan he never had the chance to actually cast. His notebooks abound with ways to make life easier through automation—stables with mechanisms to regularly feed the horses and remove the manure, armored assault vehicles that ran themselves, automatic weaving mechanisms, machines that harvested the wind and water, on and on, each aspect of which was rendered, from multiple perspectives, with a care to detail unheard of in previous engineering logs. In effect, he taught the continent how to properly and thoroughly carry out a technical drawing, setting a standard for precision, clarity, and detail that we are still chasing to some degree.

While monarchs planned grand projects to glorify themselves or to produce profitable land, Leonardo dreamed up ideal living communities that would improve sanitation, reduce disease (Italy was still regularly wracked with plague in da Vinci's time), and reduce crowding. While the philosophers were at work trying to create hard philosophical distinctions between humans and the rest of nature, Leonardo filled pages with diagrams from the dozens of autopsies he carried out on humans with the aim of comparing human internal structures to animal ones. And just as his engineering diagrams ushered in a new era of technical drawing, so were his anatomical diagrams the most accurate representations to be found anywhere until centuries after his death.

Yet, as perhaps had to happen to a person so out of step with his time, Leonardo failed more often than he succeeded. The number of his unfinished paintings runs even with those he completed, while his drive for experimentation and improvement hastened the deterioration of his finished products. His great bronze horse couldn't be completed when the needed bronze was recalled for use in casting cannons. (Michelangelo, always spoiling for a fight, would later throw this failure in Leonardo's face during a public argument.) His plan to capture a besieged city peacefully through a redirection of its water supply proved a lengthy and costly debacle. And, most psychologically disturbing, he never mastered flight in spite of years devoted to its study.

And that is the great, tragic theme of Leonardo's life: his yearning unconsummated. What you see in his notebooks is a man spending every piece of himself trying to learn everything in the universe, so that he'll finally see how it all hangs together, and never finding satisfaction. You see him

master the sum total of a discipline's knowledge, only to lash out at himself for still not having the unifying answers he sought. He was, in his own estimation, a case study in perpetual failure, redeemed only by being aware of how much he had yet to learn. For priests and astrologers, who pretended to complete knowledge, he had nothing but contempt: "Many are those who trade in tricks and simulated miracles, duping the foolish multitude; and if nobody unmasked their subterfuges, they would impose them on everyone."

No church, no god, would stand in the way of Leonardo's quest for answers. He worked on Sundays and cast scorn on those who would place arbitrary dogmatic limitations on man's quest for knowledge. He seems not to have believed in an afterlife and was, according to Vasari, a heathen by reputation. In his religious paintings, traditional symbolism is eschewed to make way for moments of human truth. His *Virgin Mary* is a mother, playing simply with her child. His *Adoration of the Magi* is as notable for the novelty of its compositional approach as for the artist's self-representation at the picture's edge, gazing away from the commotion, pondering his own world entirely. Convents and patrons could ask for all the cherubim and traditional symbols they wanted, Leonardo would follow his own muse, and represent the mysteries of existence according to his own brilliant but troubled soul.

Of course, in between moments of brilliance and despair, there was a lot of partying. The Italian fifteenth and early sixteenth centuries were punctuated with manic celebrations organized by wealthy mercantile families aiming to display their

dominance and pacify the commoners. And Leonardo relished it. He curled his beard and wore fine, rose-colored shirts, devised elaborate pranks, and surrounded himself with beautiful people (for that matter he was himself, by all accounts, strikingly handsome to the end of his days). Often disgusted with people (most, he once wrote during a dark moment, were little more than walking intestinal tracts), he nevertheless was obsessed with being useful and pleasing to them. Those periods when he had no practical or amusing work to perform, such as his dismal stay in Rome, were among the saddest of his life.

And so his reputation grew, as the man who knew everything, whose conversation held wonders, who was as gorgeous to look upon as his works were awesome to behold, who could play a lute as flawlessly as he could render a face, and who could be relied upon to strain every nerve of his electric brain to find ways to improve your life, if you would let him. As such, he was sought after by the greatest figures of Italian history—Lorenzo de Medici and Ludovico Sforza, Isabella d'Este and Cesare Borgia, Niccolo Machiavelli and Francis I, all lent him their protection and patronage at one point or another. His last protector, Francis I of France, paid all of his expenses just for the pleasure of his conversation, to be able to listen to the great man explain his understanding of the world.

Albertus Magnus, Peter Abelard—these are figures we moderns will never feel entirely at home with, and our descendants even less so. Their words and worries, hopes and decisions, are swathed in a psychological lexicon that takes a conscious act of imaginative abstraction to grasp, so as much as we admire them we never feel that they are of us. That is not the case with Leonardo. I suspect he will be as warmly welcomed into the sympathies of humans in 2216 as now, his fevered need to Do and Know Everything resonating with something inside all of us who know that time on this planet is short and precious, while his empathy with all living things and overriding need to be useful to his fellow humans can only grow in attractiveness as we make the turn from creatures unified by religion to people sharing an interest in each other. We'll feel at home with his darkness, as we'll feel exulted by his moments of synthesis, and we shall always, I imagine, feel his secure hand pushing us forward, to learn what he could not. His notebooks are our spiritual home, and will be so long as there is a universe to question.

FURTHER READING

There is a bit written about Leonardo. In English, two classic works are by Kenneth Clark (1939, revised 1967) and Serge Bramly (1988), either of which will do you well as an overview of Leonardo's life, though they necessarily can't include some of the more recent Leonardo discoveries, like the Isabella d'Este portrait that finally surfaced in 2013. Then it's a good idea to head into his notebooks themselves—there are some neat collections out there which strive to put together in categories the thoughts which Leonardo scrawled haphazardly through seven thousand pages of surviving text and drawing. There are even several free versions of the text available to you pad-owners out there, meaning you could start engaging with Leonardo's brain Right Now!

Farewell, the Soul Immortal: The Reality-First Psychology of Pietro Pomponazzi

BOLOGNA, 1518.

SO, PIETRO POMPONAZZI- YOU THINK HUMANS AREN'T IMMORTAL? THAT'S KIND OF A DOWNER.

WELL, *SORRY*, BUT EVERYTHING MEANINGFUL ABOUT OUR IDENTITY IS ULTIMATELY TIED TO THE BODY, WHICH WE KNOW PERISHES UTTERLY.

BUT I REALLY *WANT* TO BE IMMORTAL!

I REALLY WANT A LUCK DRAGON, BUT ONLY A FOOL PINES AFTER THE IMPOSSIBLE.

WAIT, HOW DO *YOU* KNOW ABOUT LUCK DRAGONS?

WELL, I WAS RUNNING AWAY FROM THESE BULLIES...

NEVER MIND- LISTEN, IF WE'RE MORTAL, DOESN'T THAT TAKE AWAY ALL OF OUR INCENTIVE TO, LIKE, BE GOOD AND STUFF?

ALWAYS THINKING LIKE AN INDIVIDUAL. LOOK, HUMANS ARE ENTWINED WITH OTHER HUMANS- WE ARE GOOD BECAUSE GOODNESS IS ITS OWN REWARD, AND ONCE WE STOP BELIEVING IN AN AFTERLIFE, MAYBE WE CAN BE *ACTUALLY* GOOD FOR THE FIRST TIME, INSTEAD OF JUST *CALCULATINGLY* GOOD. UNDERSTAND?

NOPE!

UMMM... THE FIRST RULE OF BEING A BRO IS TO BE A BRO?

UNDERSTOOD COMPLETELY!

mmortality. For twelve hundred years, we had it. As the stoic realism of the Romans faded away, it left in its wake a heady neo-Platonic dualism that preached the metaphysical otherness, and therefore deathlessness, of the human soul. We knew nothing so surely as that there was a life beyond this one, and that there our true reward or punishment was to be had. We built cavernous and desperately self-contradictory theologies to buttress that notion, and pretended to our utmost that all was well. And, for over a thousand years, it worked, until a Mantuan Aristotelian named Pietro Pomponazzi (1462-1525) blew over the entire philosophical house of cards with one swift, devastating breath.

He was simultaneously the Last of the Scholastics and the First of the Moderns, pushing through a rigorous and critical investigation of the basic assumptions of medieval theology at one moment while erecting a new human-centered but classically inspired system of morality, will, and purpose at another. Over the course of a few decades and five books, he wrote the first rigorous critiques of personal immortality, prayer, miracles, and theological morality, but draped in an Aristotelian language so compelling that the religious authorities of his time could do little more than huff and harrumph at his lack of discretion while leaving him personally free to teach as he wished.

To understand why he was able to get away with such radical views in the teeth of the Inquisition's golden years, we have to peer into the theories of the soul that preceded him. Aristotle had been pretty clear that the soul is just the form of the body, intimately tied to it in every meaningful way. This was, of course, not what the first Christian philosophers wanted to hear, and so early in the game they started injecting Platonism into the body of Christian thought, keeping Aristotle's teachings on logic and argumentation, while slowly importing the idea of the soul as a substance separate from, and superior to, the body.

It was the birth of dualism, and it was a sloppy mess from the start. Yes, it allowed for personal immortality, as everything fundamental about us was shifted to the soul, which was free to operate once the body was gone, but on a mechanical level it didn't make a bit of sense even in the hands of its most deft of theorists. How an immaterial, formal soul interfaced with a material body, how the material world was able to produce changes and development in something immaterial, how differences in personality were to be accounted for, these and a cavalcade of other questions were the issues that perplexed the greatest of the medieval philosophers, and their answers were all, unilaterally, unsatisfactory upon the scantest inspection.

However, so great was the need for immortality in the Christian system, and so powerful the church that insisted upon the absolute certainty of personal immortality, that the whole philosophical catastrophe was allowed to limp along, under-scrutinized, for *centuries*. The two dominant versions of the soul that Pomponazzi had to grapple with were those of Averroes and St. Thomas Aquinas. And grapple with them he did, with a ruthless insistence on rigor that the soul hadn't faced since Roman times.

Both Averroes and Aquinas had, in their own ways, deepened the tradition of separating the soul and intellect from the body, and therefore carving out a bit of potential space for personal immortality. For Averroes, all men partook of a common reservoir of intelligence that stood outside of space and time, while St. Thomas, admitting that the soul did seem to depend rather much on the body, hypothesized nonetheless that the most important part of it was wholly separate in nature, and could live on beyond our death. Pomponazzi, however, wasn't having any of that. His mantra was the investigation of the mind and psychology of man As We Experience It, not as we theorize it to be.

Looked at from this point of view, he argued, it is eminently clear that there is nothing in the content of our interaction with the world, not even those lofty moments when we are thinking about thinking, or considering abstract objects, which does not, at its base, have some link with our material natures. How we see and feel, how we generalize and fantasize, are all based on events that are fundamentally materially mediated. Who we are, then, is linked entirely to our physical being, and, whatever existence one might hypothesize persists after death, the conclusion must be that it is of a type wholly different from that which we know, and that therefore the individual who experiences such an afterlife is, in no recognizable or meaningful way, ourselves.

When we die, we die. Everything that forms our character as it stands is connected to physicality, and with the perishing of the body comes the end of anything that could possibly resemble ourselves. There is no heaven, no hell, no afterlife, no ultimate reward. There is just the time we have now, and every attempt to philosophically prove otherwise is based on abstract speculation that has no grounds in life as it is actually led.

The book in which Pomponazzi laid out these claims, *De immortalitate animae* (1516), made him a name Europe-over. While some copies were ritually burned by the church, the only official action the Vatican took was to have counter-texts written and published, which Pomponazzi deftly swatted down in his *Apologia* and *Defensorium*.

To the arguments that humans *must* be immortal, because (a) they yearn after immortality, and surely God wouldn't allow a yearning that couldn't be satisfied, (b) the unpunished wickedness and unrewarded virtue of this world have to be respectively punished and rewarded *somewhere*, if God is to be considered just, (c) morality would fall apart without it, and (d) as a matter of fairness, life being too short to reach our goals, as part of God's magnanimity, there must be an extended life beyond this one, Pomponazzi had several ingenious responses that prefigure much of our modern humanist canon.

As to our yearning after immortality, Pomponazzi's response was, in a nutshell, "Suck it up." We yearn after all sorts of things we can't have because we have a capacity to form abstract concepts from concrete situations. We live, and can *imagine* a longer life, and therefore yearn after it. But that's on us, and our lack of proper perspective. Only a fool feels bad because he can't have the un-haveable. And only a greater fool would build a whole philosophical system on the necessity of its haveability.

On a less smack-talking level, Pomponazzi's new system of morality and purpose is a brilliant stroke of perspective switching. Yes, mortality means no heaven, and it also means that you'll only get to do a fraction of the things you wanted to do. But, you're not alone. You are part of a species that is constantly changing and advancing and meeting collective goals that are far beyond what you could do even given an eternity of self-development. Rather than moping that you didn't get to master every skill ever in your short decades of life, learn to take satisfaction in contributing to the big project of man. Instead of feeling bad that you won't, on this earth, be a genius or a master craftsman, perfect that which is in everybody's power to perfect, namely your capacity for *goodness*. Not everybody can be brilliant, but everybody can work towards being good, and when immortality is removed from the picture, that goodness will be its own source of satisfaction, untinged by the baseness of Ultimate Reward, just as your occasional episodes of not-so-good behavior will cause real and fundamental self-reflection, instead of being sloughed off in ritualized penance.

Rather than seeing mortality as the death knell of morality, Pomponazzi recasts it as the fundamental criterion for any morality worth having, and in that recasting there is the script for the whole project of modern secular behavior. That we are wired to receive satisfaction from social good is a psychological fact Pomponazzi, alone amongst the Scholastics, appreciated. And the view of human potential, detangled from the bonds of eternity, is pretty inspiring stuff still.

But wait, that's not all! For Pomponazzi took his naturalist investigations a step further, into the realm of miracles, prayers, and prophecy, in a set of books published only after his death. He insisted with unflagging vigor that everything that had ever been described as supernatural in origin was either the work of profit-hungry charlatans or the result of a natural, if currently unknowable, set of causes. Granted, these causes included chains of astrological influence that we wouldn't accept as entirely rigorous today, but the whole thrust of Pomponazzi's inquiry was a bold departure, insisting that the myriad of angels and demons that common belief had interfering on a constant basis in the affairs of men was nothing but vulgar superstition covering a lack of knowledge about the causal changes behind the seemingly miraculous.

There are dodgy bits in these works, but his section on prayer is priceless. Basically, on Pomponazzi's account, it doesn't do anything. Event A is going to happen whether you pray for it to come about or not. There's no changing the mind of God or the universe by Really Wanting Something. At best, you're giving yourself some spare moments of reflection to think about the things you want to improve in your life, a bit of space to question what it is you need and what it is you merely desire, which is useful in making you a better person, but certainly not a causal universe-disrupting power (though he does ponder the possibility of there being a mechanical ability of a brain, concentrating hard enough, to alter its surroundings—a bit Jean Grey, sixteenth-century style).

Against a continent-wide philosophy that said, unequivocally, we are immortal souls clad in temporary bodies, bound for heaven or hell, and in constant effective contact with the divine, Pomponazzi raised a sole but powerful call for sober reflection, a fundamental investigation a millennium past-due of what life actually looks like. We shall die, but can still be happy, and good, and wise, and if the heavens won't turn at our command, we can take satisfaction in each other, and learn at long last contentment from those virtues within our power to perfect.

FURTHER READING

The last book in English that dealt solely and systematically with his thought was 1910's *The Philosophy and Psychology of Pietro Pomponazzi* by Halliday Douglas. Luckily, that is readily available as a historical reprint through Forgotten Books. His main book, *On the Immortality of the Soul*, is available in English translation in *The Renaissance Philosophy of Man* collection by Cassirer, and in Latin all over the place.

Keeping It Real: The Pragmatic Religious Skepticism Of Niccolò Machiavelli

Perhaps misrepresenting Machiavelli is a deep necessity of human civilization. We need a totem for intellect married to ruthlessness, and he has filled that role for so long that, even though we've long since discovered how unjust a portrayal it is, we've kept to it out of pure mental inertia. Niccolò Machiavelli (1469-1527) was an anti-Christian, bisexual, republican poet who wrote some of the best comedies of the Italian Renaissance. But all we ever hear is that *The Prince* was a very wicked book about how thumping good fun being a tyrant is, written by a very wicked man.

As history lovers, perpetuating that stereotype is bad enough, but as humanists it's unforgivable, because it was Machiavelli who first posed the question, in its starkest terms, "What good is religion? Why do we keep it around?" In a time when people were still hotly debating the truth of Christianity's fundamental principles, Machiavelli's approach was a frank, "Listen, we all know that people make up the religion that suits them. So let's stop pretending to truth and start talking about social utility." As a religious analyst, he wasn't quite a Marxist *avant la lettre*, but he was damn close.

He was also unemployed for over half of his life. His father came from a respectable and wealthy family, but disdained the commerce that was Florence's lifeblood. He lived off the meager income from his inheritance, his only extravagance a magnificent collection of the Latin classics. He was a bookish layabout who dabbled in law, and his son learned from his example. Niccolò didn't have a real job until he was twenty-nine years old. In the meantime, he wrote poetry, studied the central works of the Tuscan vernacular tradition, and watched the great events of Florence's history from the sidelines.

Politically, the late fifteenth century was a galloping confusion. The years from 1490 to 1512 alone saw Florence ruled by the Medici family, then by a religious zealot, then by a middle class republican council, then by the Medici family again. Meanwhile, war loomed ever present as the warrior popes led armies to conquer new territories and the French and Habsburgs fought over which would invade northern Italy next.

Machiavelli watched the frothing chaos and drew some stark conclusions about how inadequate whimsical political theory was when thrown into the cauldron of harsh reality. In 1498 he finally obtained a chancery post after the Florentines overthrew the grim religious oligarchy of Savonarola, and maintained that post until 1512, when his association with republicanism made him *persona non grata* with the returned Medici clan. He was ejected from his office, tortured, and released to what would be eight years of unemployment, poverty, and unparalleled creativity.

The first product of his exile was *The Prince*, a book as famous as it is misunderstood. It was written at a time when the Medici were trying to expand their influence into former papal territories, lands which had no experience with political equality or representative government. *The Prince* is, ultimately, a book of advice for what a ruler should do when attempting to govern a city possessing stark and time-worn social inequalities.

The advice is shocking, there is no doubt. As opposed to the idealist Ciceronian ethics of upright morality and absolute honesty, Machiavelli proposes a somber realist ethic benefiting from his observations of Italian political disorder and the meteoric career of Cesare Borgia. Eschewing high-flown theory, he describes how things happen in the real world. To succeed as the ruler of a broken land, you have to have the *appearance* of virtue while allowing yourself the luxury of timely deceit. You have to be ruthless without being hated, pious without being religious. You must be constantly preparing against disaster, because it *will* come. Sure, you can attempt to be a nice guy, to introduce popular legislation that expands governmental inclusivity, but as soon as you begin, you will be swallowed alive by the twisting social contradictions of the system you're attempting to modernize, and other cities will seize the opportunity of profiting from the resultant turmoil.

Ultimately, Machiavelli's advice in *The Prince* boils down to, "If you're ruling a broken and corrupt land, and you want to keep ruling it, you need to be a bit broken and ruthless yourself." He was definitely not saying that every city everywhere needed to be ruled by a ruthless tyrant, and the proof of that lies in his next book, *Discourses on the First Decade of Livy*. This book was a republican manifesto, extolling the superior virtue and liveliness of a city governed by republican equality rather than monarchical whim. It praised civic strife, the rough and tumble of free, even acrimonious, debate, as a spur to growth and improvement. Contrasting the golden age of the Roman Republic, when the people were in charge of their own governance, and formed militias to fight their own battles, with the modern Italian age, when the greed of the Catholic Church keeps Italy fragmented and dependent on foreign mercenaries for its defense, Machiavelli argues strenuously for a return to the civic vigor of a widely representative government.

Taken together, *The Prince* and the *Discourses* couldn't be clearer: a representative, republican government is by far the best, but if you are in a position of having to rule a land that has spent centuries actively stomping out public discourse, forcing instant governmental equality by decree will rip the state apart.

The *Discourses* also contains some of the most frank passages about the role of religion in civilization that have ever been put to paper. Starting with ancient Rome, Machiavelli notes how Numa Pompilius improved on Romulus's state by, essentially, pretending to be inspired by a nymph. He used religion as a vehicle for social con-

trol, and that is Machiavelli's fundamental take on what religion is all about. Forget about truth, forget about the *actual* attributes of God, the real question is, what sort of religion is the most useful for creating the most vigorous populace? At a stroke, he wipes all the metaphysical superstructure that Christianity had been building for a millennium and a half off the board, and shines a searing light on the craven power structure beneath.

Paganism, with its vigorous ethic of personal excellence, created people capable of astounding things. Not believing in an

afterlife, they sought their grandeur in the world. Christianity, however, by focusing on the afterlife and on the cultivation of servility before God and humility before power, has created a continent that has given up on itself. Europe generally and Italy in particular were, Machiavelli felt, drifting aimlessly along the tides of their own indifferent decadence, stirring only when absolute disaster loomed, and the blame for that listlessness he placed at the feet of Christianity.

This baseline irreverence became out and out parody when Machiavelli turned his hand to the writing of dramatic comedy. His greatest work for the stage, *Mandragola,* is a cynical *tour de force* of lust and deceit, all aided and abetted by a magnificently corrupt man of the cloth. At one point, a character shrugs off damnation with the lines, "The worst that can happen to you is to die and go to hell, and many others have suffered the same fate—many gentlemen, too! Are you ashamed to be damned with such company as them?" Heaven for the weather, hell for the company.

Meanwhile, Machiavelli's personal correspondence was filled with references to his manifest lack of personal piety. When he was commissioned to find a preacher by the Lenten Wool Guild, his friend Guicciardini chortled that it was akin to somebody asking Pacchierotto, Florence's most renowned homosexual, to choose a beautiful bride for a friend. In the Victorian age, Machiavelli and a number of other Renaissance figures underwent a religious whitewashing. Fictional accounts of deathbed conversions abounded and pious documents were forged. It took a good century to uncover the real Florence from these encrusted holy lies, and now we see the Renaissance for what it was: an era of widespread religious

skepticism, with Machiavelli's pragmatic recasting of Christianity at its heart.

By 1520, Machiavelli had done his time as an outcast, and the Medici were ready to use his talents again. He was enlisted to write a comprehensive history of Florence, from antiquity down to the modern day. The *Florentine Histories* which resulted were predictably pro-republic and as anti-Medici as Machiavelli felt he could get away with under the circumstances. Here, as in the *Discourses,* he showed how Florence was at its best when the people were allowed to thrash out their own path, and at its weakest when ruled by the contradictory whims of pseudo-monarchs like Cosimo or Lorenzo de Medici. When he wasn't writing, he was rushing around Italy as a military advisor to the forces attempting to stave off the latest threat of Habsburg invasion.

Respected for his political insight, honored for the products of his pen, and beloved for his raucous comedies, Machiavelli's final years were the culmination of a long, hardscrabble existence. He had written (but not published) the most notorious book of political philosophy of all time, and shattered the comfortable illusions of political idealism and religious metaphysics. Exhausted with Italian turmoil, he reduced the religious governance of men to questions of fundamental utility and cultural context, a perspective shift that would have to wait until Hegel, Feuerbach, and Marx three centuries later to realize its full potential. He gave us practical, rather than merely rhetorical, reasons to believe in republican equality, and asked questions of religion that cut past a thousand ponderous subtleties to place belief in the context of power and control. The least we can do in return is stop using the word "Machiavellian" as a pejorative. So, the next time a world leader does something ruthless and cunning, instead of describing him as Machiavellian, say, "Man, that dude is *so* Borgian."

Because Cesare Borgia? That guy was an ass.

FURTHER READING

Machiavelli is one of the most written-about figures in world intellectual history, and the last ten years in particular have seen a flood of books about him and his work. The most recent, *Machiavelli: A Portrait* (2015) by Christopher Celenza somehow manages to be both very brief and highly padded. The book is just a smidge over two hundred tiny pages, and yet feels the need to fill space with long side-tracks into matters not particularly relevant to the life of Machiavelli, and maddening repetition. You'll do far better to go back another couple of years to *Machiavelli* (2013) by Robert Black. Black has spent three decades mired in Machiavelli scholarship, and it shines forth from every page of his definitive account. There are sections that you might not be particularly interested in (Black can spend two pages in virtuosic source-wrangling trying to pin down whether a book was begun in 1514 or 1515), but the portrayal of Machiavelli's radical novelty and intellectual daring is intoxicating.

A Note on the Comic

Yes, Machiavelli wouldn't have known about the contents of *The Prince* or the *Discourses* in 1498, as he hadn't written them yet. But he's obviously been visited by enough time-travelers that he's picked up the details of what he *will* write, so it's okay.

The Reformation's One Good Man:
Erasmus of Rotterdam

For half a millennium, in spite of all the towering thinkers that have come since, and all the ones we're furiously brewing today, when we talk about *the* humanist we all picture the same guy: Erasmus of Rotterdam (1466-1536), the man whose arguments for basic decency, thorough scholarship, and general affability ended up sparking a cavalcade of bloodshed he would repudiate. Through his wit and discerning eye, the Renaissance became the Reformation, and two hundred years of steady progress gave way to a hundred and fifty of sustained manic horror. Erasmus is proof that great ideas, be they ever so benignly stated, and offered with the best of intentions, are rarely unaccompanied by profound grief.

The man who would become the most celebrated scholar of his age had perhaps the fifteenth century-est origin ever. He was the illegitimate son of a priest. His mother died of the plague. Upon the subsequent death of his father (probably also of the plague), he was thrust against his will into a monastery by his shameless guardians. The only thing missing is a subplot involving poisoning at the hands of an Italian named Niccolo Stabieri.

Erasmus later painted his time as a monk in the darkest colors, but in many ways it was the best place for him. There he had the leisure to cultivate his manifold classical geekeries, devouring Latin authors and developing his own immaculate prose style while forging gushing romantic friendships with his fellow monks. At the waning end of the Renaissance, monasteries were often little more than Antiquity Enthusiast clubs, a fact that infuriated the dour and joyless foot soldiers of the coming Reformation, but that was perfect for the sickly, sensitive, bookish Erasmus.

As much as his later public persona was that of the modest and retiring intellectual, Erasmus was, in fact, all about The Fame. When a chance came to ditch the monastery and travel to Paris, he grabbed it and spent the rest of his life resolutely not being a monk. The coming years saw him perpetually broke but leveraging his imposing erudition into a towering intellectual reputation that spanned the continent. When the times grew too lean, or plague threatened, he'd escape to England where the academic scene was more welcoming under the direction of a not-yet-executed Thomas More.

Erasmus was becoming a name. He collected and published the *Adagia* in 1500, a massive reference of Latin quotes to inspire the pens of the ineloquent. For an emerging publishing market dominated by Latin, it was an indispensable volume and Erasmus would continue releasing expanded editions of it for the rest of his life.

That same love of language pushed him to learn Greek, a knowledge of which brought him up against the cold hard fact that the Vulgate, the Catholic Church's approved Latin translation of the Bible, was a sticky mess of corruptions and misguided philology. So, very innocently, he set about the task of *fixing* the Bible, and in 1516 came out with the *Novum Instrumentum omne,* a New Testament with Greek text and an extensive commentary which pointed out contradictions, linguistic obscurities, and irretrievable corruptions, all in the most open and helpful spirit.

Political astuteness was not then, any more than it is now, the outstanding attribute of the cloistered classicist. What Erasmus took to be a humble academic offering the religious community considered dangerous and borderline heretical.

Many in the church did not take at all well to having their central religious text held up as a philologically suspect mass of lost meanings and encrusted but misinformed tradition. When Erasmus said he happily sought original meaning, an increasingly defensive church heard its textual infallibility and constancy challenged, and the rising generation of Reformers took note. When Luther produced his German Bible, it was from Erasmus's text.

It wasn't the first time Erasmus's light intentions were taken amiss by a ponderous and neurotic religious establishment. In 1511, Erasmus had written his bestseller, his masterpiece, the book that keeps his name alive while all his contemporaries have faded into utter obscurity: *Praise of Folly*. It was a lark, tossed off in a few days to amuse his friend, Thomas More. Its silliness is profound, its self-mockery magnificent, and its airy intellectual spaciousness is the last of its kind before Europe got swallowed by the glum and cavernous wailings of Lutheranism. It's the literary equivalent of a cool breeze through summer leaves in which Folly makes its case as the real basis of everything pleasant in life.

Erasmus argues in the face of all learned tradition for the simple human beauty of self-deception, of purely subjective pleasure-taking. If your wife is beautiful *to you*, that's all that matters. If a group of people is enjoying something silly and superficial, let them, because there's nothing more noxious than a morbid self-seriousness that refuses to bend to the occasion.

He takes devastating shots at perpetual academics like himself and at the resplendent absurdities of traditional religious practice and the priesthood. His is a vision of bourgeois mental delight—of simplicity in religion, depth in friendship, and a willingness to let one's self be goofy and a bit blind if it helps people get along pleasantly with one another. It is the best and last summation of the joyful spirit of antiquity, and within six years it was a spiritual outcast to its times.

For 1517 brought Luther, the Ninety-five Theses, and the whole macabre mechanism of shame and sin that was the European Reformation. Catholics and Protestants alike doubled down on the most restrictive and abhorrent of their beliefs about humanity's nature and purpose, and both sought Erasmus, the most famous intellectual of his day, for support.

Initially sympathetic to Luther's cause, Erasmus was soon appalled by its excesses, the burning of churches and the waging of wars. In his luscious naivety, he thought the massive issues at hand could be resolved by a friendly chat, and never understood the real depth of the issues at stake. Himself a first-caliber book nerd, he couldn't comprehend that the Reformation was about something more than the role of classicism in religion.

From being the master and summit of a continent's intellectual life, he became a grasping spectator, his rambling defenses and descent into Catholic conservatism painfully demonstrating his advancing age and disillusionment. He still wrote religious texts that satisfied nobody in that polarized age, authoritative collections of the church fathers, and at least one sally back into the laughing spirit of better days, the *Colloquia*. He was still read and consulted. But his last two decades were a bitter march plagued by a horde of imaginary, and a few quite real, intellectual adversaries over whom he wasted a frankly depressing amount of life and ink.

As much as the real Erasmus tapered to a bitter end, the original Erasmus, the frothy author of *Praise of Folly*, lingered on past his death, influencing the heady climate of intellectual freedom in the Dutch Republic that became the benchmark for self-deprecating tolerance for all of Europe, and thence for us, inspiring our most dearly held and emotionally sacred national motto: "Be excellent to each other, and party on, dudes."

FURTHER READING

Praise of Folly is available everywhere, and is one of the prime examples of an author's most famous book also being his best book. In its adamant refusal to knuckle under to long-standing philosophical prejudices, it's unlike anything else in the standard European canon. It is also perhaps the single most pleasant book in the Western philosophical tradition. *Colloquia* is also available here and there, but it is more of a specialized dish. It consists of a series of short vignettes composed to demonstrate how to construct different dialogue scenes in Latin, and jumps between humorous shorts to scathing critiques of Erasmus's personal enemies to long paragraphs detailing, for example, fifty different ways to say, "We haven't seen you for a while" in Latin. The rest of Erasmus's published work is composed of letters, of interest to historians, classical compendia, of interest to linguists, and commentaries on psalms and church fathers, of interest to, let's be honest here, essentially nobody. For books about Erasmus, I like Johan Huizinga's *Erasmus and the Age of Civilization* (1924) a great deal. It doesn't shy away from Erasmus's vanity, indecision, and occasional cruelty to his friends, but also doesn't fail to give lavish praise where it's due. For Erasmus and those who influenced him, *Humanists and Jurists: Six Studies in the Renaissance* (1963) by Myron P. Gilmore is a nice, brisk introduction.

Out-Princing the Princes: The Renaissance Patronage and Diplomacy of Isabella d'Este

MANTUA, 1502.

DEAREST ISABELLA, CONSOLE ME! THE *WICKED* BORGIA HAS INVADED MY CITY AND TURNED US, ITS RIGHTFUL RULERS, OUT!

THERE, THERE, BELOVED ELISABETTA!

AND HE HAS STOLEN ALL OUR PRICELESS ART AS WELL!

HAS HE?

YOU!

ME?

YES. THE DUCHESS HAS AN *EXQUISITE* SET OF VENUS AND CUPID STATUES IN HER COLLECTION. QUICKLY, RIDE TO BORGIA'S CAMP AND ASK IF HE'LL GIVE THEM TO ME, AS A TOKEN OF ESTEEM.

OKAY, BUT I'M SUPPOSED TO BE LEARNING A LIFE LESSON HERE...

BEGONE!

THERE'S LIKE SHOWVALIS

OH, SISTER-IN-LAW, DID I HEAR THAT YOU WILL USE YOUR INFLUENCE WITH THE BORGIAS TO RECLAIM MY BELOVED STATUES?

YES!

TO THEN RETURN TO ME IN MY HOUR OF GRIEF?

OH, LOVE, OF *COURSE* NOT!

I ALREADY HAVE A SPOT PICKED OUT FOR THEM IN MY *NOT*-PLUNDERED ART GROTTO, AND BY FORGING A PERSONAL TIE WITH CESARE BORGIA THROUGH THE EXCHANGE, I'M MAKING SURE MANTUA ISN'T THE NEXT CITY TO BE CASUALLY SACKED.

AND *THAT'S* HOW YOU DO RENAISSANCE DIPLOMACY.

BOOM.

Bald-faced treachery has always been a stalwart component of European statesmanship, but there was one era, and one nation, that elevated it to *the* central principle of all diplomacy worth the name—Renaissance Italy. Pope and Borgia, emperor and Medici, along with every city-state that could field two dozen ramshackle soldiers, formed and dissolved alliances with a cynical relish curbed by neither family ties nor honor. As a result, the threat of attack and siege was part of every city's routine waking existence. Every city, except one.

Mantua. It raised excellent horses, and that was more or less it. And yet, during the time that Urbino was sacked (twice), Milan was invariably being ruled by a French puppet, the pope strapped on armor to led an army to conquer Bologna, and the Medicis rose, fell, and rose again in Florence, Mantua remained untouched, thanks almost entirely to the keen statesmanship of its *de facto* ruler, the irrepressible Isabella d'Este (1474-1539).

She was born in 1474, in Ferrara, to a ruling family that worshipped literature and the arts as the summits of human expression, and particularly anything springing from pagan antiquity. She was given free rein in the magnificent d'Este palaces, with their overflowing bookshelves and art-saturated walls, and absorbed it all so readily that, before even entering into her teenage years, she was renowned throughout Italy for the depth of her culture and quickness of conversation.

Her family held onto her as long as they could, but eventually had to surrender her to the arranged marriage that had been contracted when she was a child, to the Mantuan heir, Francesco Gonzaga. He was a brave soldier, but a hopelessly outclassed diplomat with zero ability to artfully dissemble, and a penchant for serial infidelity. Had Francesco ruled on his own, Mantua would have been the hapless plaything of greater powers. Fortunately, while he was away, playing soldier for Venice, or the pope, or whoever needed a man in an impressive doublet to bark orders at genetically treacherous troops, Isabella remained behind, forming a network of friends and informers that would secure the safety of Mantua while at the same time earning her reputation as the greatest humanist patron of the early sixteenth century.

And that is why she is remembered, if she is remembered, now. Her diplomatic achievements, while stunning, are obscure and complicated to modern ears, employing influences with third cousins and well-placed courtiers to neutrally straddle temporary alliances just long enough to spring to the next big thing. But, her patronage has left us some of the unambiguously great masterpieces of human fancy. In painting, she supported Mantegna, Leonardo, Raphael, Titian, Perugino, Bellini, and Costa. In literature, she backed a publication project to produce a collected edition of all the known works of antiquity, sent her son to study with the great skeptic thinker (and denier of the immortality of the soul), Pietro Pomponazzi, and provided financial and emotional aid to Niccolò da Correggio, Ariosto, and a host of other Italian poets and humanist scholars who used that support to create a new, classically centered, intellectual culture in the heart of Catholicism.

In her grotto, she displayed all the works she commissioned on classical themes, as well as a startling array of antique treasures, providing a thematically unified gateway into the mythological past that was the admiration of, and inspiration for, a new generation of artists and writers. Her agents combed Italy and Greece, hunting for rarities and forging personal connections with highly placed individuals who would, in their turn, be used by Isabella as sources of political and artistic information. In many ways, it was her ceaseless stream of correspondence and patronage that rendered Isabella practically immune to the workaday treachery of the early sixteenth century. While Medici, Sforza, and Borgia stormed across Italy, allied with popes, French kings, and German emperors as opportunities presented themselves, her letters and presents, devoted ambassadors and eager informants kept her and Mantua in the good graces of all, and two steps ahead of the shifting political scene, even in the midst of near-universal ruin.

As Machiavelli wrote *The Prince* in honor of the meteoric, determined rise of Cesare Borgia, he might have more profitably turned to the diplomatic magic of Isabella d'Este, who managed to somehow simultaneously earn both Borgia's especial good will AND that of his bitterest enemies. For three decades, nobody could bring themselves to attack Isabella's Mantua, and her personal prestige was so high that it led to one of the most remarkable episodes of the Renaissance, during the sack of Rome.

The popes had been asking for a comeuppance for the better part of a half-century, expanding their role as land-hungry secular rulers until Pope Julius II decided that he might as well drop all pretense and lead his armies personally on a conquering tour through central Italy. They dethroned legitimate kings at sword-point, created cardinals to raise money for weapons, and switched allegiances with the political wind. Eventually, the Holy Roman Emperor, Charles V, had enough of the papacy's duplicity, and sent a conquering force into Italy. Unfortunately, he failed to send money to pay these troops, so after their first victory against the Italians, the soldiers formed a mob that moved onto Rome with plunder in mind.

Isabella was in Rome at the time, working on the pope to grant a cardinal's hat to her second child (he had been made a bishop at the age of fifteen, which gives a rough idea of the rigor of ecclesiastical office-granting in the Renaissance). When the approach of the riotous army was announced, she took charge, dispatching notes to the officers she knew, and gathering over two thousand refugees within the walls of her personal palace to protect against the coming onslaught.

When the invaders arrived, the horror was general. Spanish and Germans poured through the streets of Rome, violating nuns, throwing babies from windows, desecrating the most holy shrines of the Vatican, and kidnapping anybody of note to extort immense ransoms. Only one place in the city, and one group of people, were protected from the devastation—Isabella's palace, and those people seeking refuge inside. In spite of being a staunch ally of the pope, such were her personal connections with the Spanish and German officers that, directly upon the breaching of Rome's walls, her palace was assigned a contingent of German guards to ensure the safety of all inside. While 30,000 souls died in the Eternal City, Isabella, her friends, and her collection of antiquities all survived unscathed, benefactors of Isabella's lifetime of collecting friends in the most unlikely of places.

As Isabella's son, a dissipated and impetuous soldier like his father, assumed increasing control of the governance of Mantua, Isabella retired to her grotto, to bask and add to the art and ideas that she had brought into the world. She eventually assumed the rulership of a small town in Romagna that kept her organizational skills occupied to her death in 1539. Hailed as one of the greatest statesmen of her time, she has been all too easily forgotten in the intervening years. We remember the warriors, the peacekeepers, the artists, and not the patrons who gave them work and encouragement. While not above profiting from the misery of others (the episode in today's comic is just one example of many), she made it a principle never to cause misery for her friends, and *everybody* was her friend. In that idea of diplomacy, as a measured accord seeking peace above all things through open lines of communication, she left a successful example of cooperation all too little followed in the subsequent European centuries. But in her granting of affection and ducats to a collection of disparate humanists, she founded a movement that would only gain in momentum through the coming years and in that sense, she is the patron of us all.

FURTHER READING

The book to read is pretty much still Julia Cartwright's two volume biography *Isabella d'Este: Marchioness of Mantua* from 1905.
She drew heavily from Isabella's massive correspondence, and while the pages upon pages of direct quotations can get bogged down in descriptions of quaternary historical figures all of whom have basically the same name, they provide a personal glimpse into the pageantry and intricacy of Renaissance nobility that is unparalleled.
While Cartwright's book is available as an electronic book, the character recognition of the version I saw is dodgy in places.
Spend a bit more and you can get a second or third edition of the original books with their gorgeous black and white plates that makes for a much more pleasant reading experience.

Giordano Bruno and the Secret Origins of Modern Philosophy

Philosophically, the sixteenth century was a mess. The rise of Protestantism knocked a millennium's worth of self-assured theological development for a loop, opening the gates to all manner of new philosophical disciplines and roving intellectual cutpurses. Everything was up for grabs, and in the chaos some found freedom, many reaped profit, and the most daring often ended their improbable lives in tragedy. Giordano Bruno (1548-1600) was one of the latter, now known more for being burned alive at the hands of the Inquisition than for the actual content of his thought and life. For anybody interested in how modern philosophy cobbled itself together from the swirling mass of occult mysticism and scholastic rigor that preceded it, Bruno's work, composed while wandering through every major intellectual center of sixteenth-century Europe, makes an ideal starting point.

In a mere fifty-two years of life, nine of which were spent rotting in an Inquisitorial jail cell, Bruno traveled to and lectured in Venice, Rome, Naples, London, Wittenberg, Frankfurt, Paris, Toulouse, Prague, and Zurich. His intellectual deftness allowed him to fit in with Calvinists, Lutherans, Catholics, hermetic magicians, and Jews with equal felicity. His belief in an infinite universe dominated by the ideas of love and forgiveness let him listen to and learn from each of these vibrant communities, and so his works brilliantly (if somewhat over-verbosely) encapsulate the contradictions and enthusiasms of his supremely contradictory and enthusiastic century.

When Giordano Bruno was born, the Council of Trent, which had started three years before as a grand attempt to honestly address the complaints and concerns of the Protestants, was already sliding into the harshly reactionary attitude that would spark a century of war and end the lives of thousands of "heretics," Bruno included. But that would be in the future—the young Giordano (or Filippo as he was known at the time—early modern academics had a charming and infuriating habit of changing their name every fifteen damn minutes) started off his theological career most promisingly. Arriving at Naples in 1562, his astounding memory and rich language made an impression on his higher-ups, and he was shipped off to Rome to perform memory tricks for the pope.

The importance of memory is an increasingly foreign concept to a generation that, as a matter of course, carries access to the entire collected wisdom of mankind in its pocket, but in the sixteenth century, lawyers, clerics, and kings were all keenly interested in ways to boost their powers of recall as a means of bypassing the laborious process of accessing archives and their dependence on shifty librarians. A lawyer wasn't worth hiring unless he could deliver a six-hour speech from memory, and for a king or pontiff who had dozens of disparate items brought before him each day for judgment and action, a keen head was indispensable.

It should come as little surprise, then, that Bruno, after getting excommunicated for picking theological fights with the wrong friars, earned most of his bread by teaching his memory system to the rulers of whatever country his wanderings landed him in. His usual pattern was to enter a city, find a way to display his gifts of memory and fluency in mathematics for the academic elite, and then parlay that display into a teaching position or private tutorship that would last the two or three years it inevitably took him to clash with the academic establishment, call them all asses (his favorite word), write inflamed philosophical dialogues that belittled them in a manner more reminiscent of an *8 Mile* rap battle than an academic paper, and flee to greener pastures just a step ahead of the lynch mob.

What started as a sure means of survival, however, proved to be the doorway to an entire philosophical system that would synthesize a century's worth of confusion and progress into a hopeful whole before being prematurely terminated by the executioner's flames. For Bruno's memory system revolved around the construction of elaborate wheels of association that brought mathematics, language, mythology, and philosophy all together in one interrelated whole. As he refined his methods, it became clearer and clearer to him that the universe could not be as Aristotle had laid it out millennia before. If everything is connected, then there can't be unbridgeable qualitative differences between objects in the observable world. The sun, he hypothesized, must be made of the same things as the Earth, and the stars as well, all part of an interconnected atomic system whose reactions push forward the ticking of the universe. The universe, he came to realize, is an infinite construct which must be broken down to the level of the infinitesimal to be understood.

Keep in mind, he wrote these reflections a full thirty years before Galileo published his observations of the sun and Jupiter, and a century before Newton and Leibniz discovered calculus by playing with those very quantities of the infinite and infinitesimal that Bruno guessed must lie at the heart of a proper mathematical analysis of the cosmos. But what is truly remarkable is that Bruno's prescience was not at all remarkable for his time. His infinite universe was already hypothesized a century before by Nicholas of Cusa, his atomism was there in the ancient works of Democritus, and his mathematical tinkering with the infinitely small can not only be found in a nascent form in the works of Archimedes, but also in his exposure to Fabrizio Mordente, a geometer whose invention of the adjustable compass so impressed Bruno that it took him a whole *five months* to steal Mordente's ideas and then stab him in the back in a series of wickedly funny but entirely unfair pamphlets.

Bruno's was not the gift of originality, but that of synthesis. By taking all of these insights and combining them with his love of Platonic emotionality and hermetic uniformity, he created an astounding whole, the swan song of Early Modernity in its most rapturous and hopeful form. In surveying the spectrum of the cosmos through his profoundly ordered memory, Bruno saw it stretching out forever into the past, with always the same messages asserting themselves. Not Catholicism, nor even Christianity, had a unique claim to the truths of existence, but rather everyone from the Egyptian priest to the skeptical Greek made their crucial contributions, all connecting to the unity of the universe in their own ways and by their own lights. To discount their ideas because of the lack of Jesus in them Bruno found foolish and shortsighted. He had no patience with the concept of Hell as being entirely foreign to his love-bound universe, and rarely spoke of the Paradise of angels outside of how we experience it on earth through our contemplation of the infinities of existence. For Bruno, interconnection meant that all of the stuff of divinity is within each human, and so any notion of original sin or fearful gods judging our unworthy world is the foundation of political control, not genuine philosophy.

What I find astounding is that all of this borrowing and stitching together produced a conception of the universe that closely mirrors that of Spinoza's revolutionary *Ethics*, written nearly a century later, with its focus on the perfection of the infinitely complex universe and man's highest calling to contemplate it and find our own natures written therein. Perhaps, had Bruno been a bit more staid in presentation or less combative in personality, and if he had not lived in an era when Catholicism was desperately thrashing about to find its feet again, we would be looking to him rather than Spinoza as the true link between medieval and modern philosophy.

In principle, he looked forward to a religion that accepted all approaches to self-enlightenment. In fact, he wasn't above exploiting religious prejudice to get what he needed. In delivering a funeral oration to a collection of influential Lutherans, he spoke of the pope as a gorgon whose "blasphemous tongues, more numerous than the hairs of his head, assist and administer, every one of them, against God, Nature, and humanity, who infect the world for the worst with their poison of ignorance and depravity." Two years later, in the clutches of the Inquisition, he was denying the authority of his Dominican jailers to judge him, saying that he only acknowledged such authority in the person of the pope, that erstwhile world-consuming gorgon.

After nearly two decades of wandering and writing, Bruno had put enough heretical notions to paper to convict him a hundred times over. He centered an entire lecture series around 120 errors of Aristotle at a time when Aristotelian philosophy formed the core of Catholic theology. He quoted obscure Egyptian texts and pre-Socratic Greek philosophers with the same frequency as Thomas Aquinas or Peter Lombard. He hypothesized a heliocentric infinite universe made of the same fundamental elements as the Earth, all in constant flux, capable of generating its own compounds and even life when the celestial spheres of Ptolemy were still the dogmatically accepted building blocks of the Christian universe. He wrote his philosophy as Italian dialogues and sprawling verse poems when Latin was the accepted language of academic discourse. He denied Hell and railed against religious persecution as contrary to the unified, love-permeated cosmos that he felt must be the true font of existence. Further, since we are all made of the same stuff, and are constantly evolving into other things, then equality must be the nature of man (even if some of them are asses), and this was against not only every reigning theological notion, but every political one as well.

In the end, it wasn't his writings that landed him in the clutches of the Inquisition, but his own quarrelsome nature. After moving to Venice to take up a potentially lucrative position as a private tutor, he soon felt the itch to return to Frankfurt, the center of the publishing world at the time, to continue his writing career. His patron insisted that Bruno stay and finish teaching him the memory system he had promised. Bruno refused and started packing his bags, only to find a half dozen gondoliers grabbing him in the middle of the night and locking him in an attic. (I don't know if this is something you can still hire gondoliers to do, but I certainly hope it is.) His patron fired off a letter to the local Inquisition detailing all of Bruno's departures from Orthodoxy listed above, and more besides, and thence began Bruno's nine-year legal dance with first the Venetian, then Roman, Inquisition.

This trial ought to be an object lesson for anybody wanting to know how the Inquisition actually worked outside of its Spanish variant. Popularly considered the kangaroo court of Early Modernity, the Italian branches of the Inquisition had strict procedural protocols, rules of the game that had to be obeyed. Bruno knew these rules all too well, and was able to nimbly dance around them for the better part of a decade until he made the fatal mistake of attempting to go over the Inquisition's head, straight to the pope, for acquittal. If Bruno's life of perpetual fleeing taught him anything, it should have been that his political instincts weren't precisely the most finely honed, and yet he finally threw away his strength, theological quibbling and rules monkeying, in favor of a political gambit that was doomed to fail. The Inquisition could put up with much in the name of protocol, but a challenge to its own authority coming from within its own prison was too much. Giordano Bruno was burned to death on February 17, 1600.

FURTHER READING

Bruno's writings encompass a number of different styles, from his mammoth satirical play *The Candlemaker* to the Platonically inspired Italian Dialogues of which *The Heroic Frenzies* is the most readily available in English to his verse epic *de Rerum Natura* clone, *On the Immense and the Numberless*. The language is what you would expect from a sixteenth-century Italian—florid and emotional and never content to use one word where a list of ten synonyms is at hand. Be prepared for long sections praising himself, and longer, but much funnier ones, decrying the asininity of everybody who disagrees with him. I'd start with *Frenzies* and see how you like it— some find the mixture of poetry and dialogue enchanting, others distracting, but it certainly is a literary experience Of Its Time, and that's worth treating yourself to now and then. Also, the Cambridge Edition of *Cause, Principle, and Unity* is not only valuable for the main text, but has a nice introduction to what made Bruno's philosophy so revolutionary in its time. For biographies on Bruno, the classic is by Frances B. Yates, though it definitely has an axe to grind. More recently, Ingrid Rowland's *Giordano Bruno: Philosopher / Heretic* (2008) is beautifully written and also pretty fun!

From the Midst of Massacre:
The Religious Tolerance of King Henry IV

The Mid-Sixteenth Century. You will never find a more wretched hive of scum and villainy. While the Renaissance had its share of opportunistic, treacherous black hats, there was always something identifiably human at the bottom of their machinations. After the launching of Luther's Reformation, however, a century long spasm of fanaticism twisted Europe, unleashing the blackest of blacks from the moral gray that preceded it—religiously driven murderers on a continental scale like Philip II or the Duke of Guise who thought nothing of decimating a province in the service of their God.

But if the black was unleashed, so too was the white, and the heroes of this age exhibited a humanity unknown since the most idealistic musings of ancient Greece—the noble and tragic Count Egmont, the wise and brave William the Silent, the clever and humane Elizabeth I, and possibly the greatest of them all, the man who made toleration his guiding principle in an age when bloody persecution was the banal norm, Henry of Navarre, later King Henry IV of France.

Henry of Navarre was born in 1553, when France was ripping itself apart in spurts of religious self-annihilation. Catherine de' Medici ruled France on behalf of her indecisive and weak-willed son, Charles IX. Her goal was to perpetuate her family's rule, and her strategy was simple and effective—she kept her rivals in a perpetual state of holy civil war that consumed their resources and attention, each peace merely a cynical stepping stone to further bloodshed. At the time, the two major families with claims to the throne were the morbidly Catholic Lorraines, controlled by the house of Guise, and the stringently Huguenot

Bourbons of Navarre. Armies of fanatics and mercenaries lumbered through the French countryside in a decade-long orgy of vengeance and destruction that depopulated entire villages in an afternoon in the name of essentially the same God.

Henry represented the Bourbon family's best chance to gain the throne, and he was given a Spartan upbringing to toughen him up towards that end. He was allowed no toys, only the most primitive food and clothing, and his teachers were forbidden to praise or flatter him. The result was that rarest of things in the sixteenth century, a child of the nobility possessed of simple interests and broad humanity. His father passed away in 1562, making him effectively the leader of the French Protestant cause at the ripe and wise age of nine.

War and intrigue were his constant companions throughout adolescence, but in 1572, an opportunity was offered him to end the bloodshed at last by marrying Catherine de' Medici's daughter. His Protestant followers told him not to go to Paris for the marriage, that it was surely a trap to gather all the Huguenot leaders together in one place for extermination, but go he did. Catherine's secret plan was to push Henry's rival, the Duke of Guise, to assassinate Henry's second in command, Admiral Coligny, thereby provoking Henry to eliminate the duke, doing away with one of Catherine's most powerful rivals. As it happened, Coligny was merely wounded, and by his explicit orders no vengeance was to be taken against the Duke of Guise.

Catherine's plan was falling apart and, caught in that moment of indecision, she resolved that the only way out was to throw her royal influence on the side of the

duke, and permit a wholesale slaughter of the Protestants. Thus began the St. Bartholomew's Day Massacre, a country-wide butchering of Huguenots to satisfy the duke's perverse religious loyalty and Catherine de' Medici's grasping cunning. Henry himself was merely placed under arrest on the promise that he would become a Catholic, but upon finally escaping he took his place at the head of the Huguenot army, renounced his conversion, and entered into alliances with England and the German Protestant princes to fight back against the oppression of the mighty, Spanish-backed Catholic League.

In the field, he was an indomitable force, wading into the thick of battle, risking his life almost recklessly, knowing that only through his own personal courage would this rag-tag collection of dour Protestants and moderate Catholics possibly continue fighting for him as a unit. He retook Catholic strongholds, always offering absolute pardon and full military honors to their vanquished defenders. Vengeance was simply not part of his nature. Even after sixteen separate attempts on his life by fanatic assassins and innumerable treacheries from those he had considered closest to him, his first instinct was always forgiveness and toleration. The death of any Frenchman, enemy or friend, grieved him: "I cannot rejoice to see my subjects lying dead upon the field. I am a loser at the very moment when I win."

Henry knew that, as long as he continued as a Protestant, the wars would continue, Frenchmen would die, and all to the benefit of hypocritical politicians and power-hungry clergymen. And so, some years after the death of the ineffectual Henry

III, who would really rather have spent his days designing clothes and wearing baskets of puppies around his neck than dealing with the intricacies of statesmanship, Henry made the decision at last to convert to Catholicism and assume the title of Henry IV.

It wouldn't end his, or France's, problems, but it gave him a platform from which to effect his country's healing. The Catholics didn't like his lenience towards the Protestants, and the Protestants abhorred how he gave all the best positions in government to Catholics in an attempt to buy their loyalty away from the Catholic League that had spent the better part of two decades gutting France for its own ends. But the country was weary of war, and glad to see a Frenchman on the throne again. And Henry had his way, guided by one of the phenomenally unsung figures of the human story, Maximilien Rosny, the eventual Duke of Sully.

Rosny was a Protestant who rose at four in the morning, worked until ten at night, and then went to bed to start the process over again. He and Henry marched in lockstep sympathy to establish a new era of toleration and justice in France. "Compassion and tenderness are the only means that do any service to religion, and the only means that religion dictates. The [religious] zeal which is so much boasted is only rage or obstinacy, disguised under a reputable appellation," he said in a condemnation of religious strife and military posturing.

While Henry ruled, Rosny governed, traveling to the countryside to witness firsthand the gross corruption of the tax machine that bled the peasants in order to fatten the collectors and their sub-contrac-

tors. With Henry's backing, he redesigned the structure of taxation, which improved revenue flow for the state while simultaneously lessening the burden of taxation for the poor. That newly found money went towards preparing a grand coalition to limit the influence of the Inquisition-fueled Habsburgs, a community of European nations that would solve problems through joint arbitration rather than war, a United Nations four centuries before its time.

When, by large-scale amnesty and unheard of bribery, Henry had brought peace to France at last, he felt established enough to produce his great legislative landmark: the 1598 Edict of Nantes, which guaranteed freedom of conscience throughout his lands, and a broad-based (though not complete) freedom of public worship with it. It stood for a century as the cornerstone of French religious policy until Louis XIV repealed it in 1685 under the influence of the drably fanatic Madame de Maintenon and his confessor François de la Chaise. In an age when you could call on huge resources by affiliating yourself strongly with one branch of Christianity or another, Henry walked a harder path, facing constant criticism and threats to his life from all sides by maintaining a policy of steady, thankless toleration.

It was what France needed, however. From the passing of the edict to his death twelve years later, France was free of religious war. The population rebounded, native industries developed, and tax revenue soared under Sully's tireless and fair watch, allowing Henry to commit resources to public projects that included a thorough reworking of sanitation systems, new roads, and public hospitals for veterans. Henry

IV was, in all ways, the king of the people, willing to accept any hardship for himself if it would mean an improvement in France's day to day lifestyle.

Wellllllll...almost any hardship. For if Henry's virtues were great, his one weakness was towering: women. Like his grandson, Charles II of England, he was pathologically incapable of monogamy, kept several mistresses simultaneously, and spent lavishly on them the money that could have gone to bolstering his plan for a European alliance. The faithful Rosny grumbled at the expense, and at having to act as intermediary between Henry, his legitimate wife (by this time, the pro-Spanish, eternally scheming Marie de' Medici, Henry having obtained papal approval for a divorce from his first wife), and his various mistresses. It was a source of eternal embarrassment to the upstanding, superhumanly moral Rosny to spend so much time soothing domestic rage, but as often as Henry would abjure his weakness and promise to reform, the next morning would see him composing letters of abject love to his various mistresses again.

As he got older, this penchant for women only grew in intensity, and his last amour was with a fifteen-year-old girl some forty-one years his junior. It was a passion so extreme that it seemed to fire every other aspect of his rule with its intensity. After two decades of preparation, he suddenly resolved to go to war against Spain to secure the freedom of Europe from Habsburg oppression, finally putting to use the money and weapons that Rosny had been storing up. At fifty-six years of age, he was set to remake the face of Europe, to bring a principle of balance that might have avoided the horrid depredations of the Thirty Years' War, when one evening a religious fanatic leapt upon him in a narrow street and stabbed him through the heart.

The age of Henry was over. For the next half century, Europe would subject itself to a destruction that would make the religious wars of Henry's youth look positively quaint by comparison, fueled by a religious zeal unchecked by compassion for humanity. The moderation of Henry and Rosny became but a memory, but the example had been set. For twenty years, Henry IV ruled France for the people, with their happiness and freedom of thought, belief, and speech his primary concerns. That memory would last, tucked away in the joint memory of the peasant classes, to emerge again in the fires of Revolution as a glimmering example of a people-centered state that had happened once and might yet happen again.

FURTHER READING

Henry is in anybody's top three list of important French rulers, and biographies and fictional portrayals aren't lacking.
For a popular account, I can't help but like Hesketh Pearson's 1963 *Henry of Navarre: The King Who Dared*. In French, I like Francois Bayrou's 1993 *Henri IV: Le Roi Libre* for its focus on the proto-republicanism of good King Henry.

From the Midst of Massacre: The Religious Tolerance of King Henry IV

Fra Paolo Sarpi: Venice's Secret Atheist?

To his contemporaries, he was an astronomer to equal Galileo. To Galileo, he was the greatest mathematician of his age. To William Harvey, he was the world's foremost expert on blood circulation. To William Gilbert, its greatest authority on magnetism. And to the pope, he was a statesman and theologian so gifted and dangerous that the only way to overcome him was via a string of stiletto-wielding assassins. In short, no matter what you did during the late sixteenth century, and no matter how brilliant you were at it, Paolo Sarpi (1552-1623) was the idol whose accomplishments you aspired to be worthy of.

And yet, until recently, he was known only as the author of a definitive history of the Council of Trent, his scientific work forgotten, his anti-papal statesmanship effectively buried by the Catholic Church, and his philosophical program all but obliterated. Then, in 1983, historian David Wootton made a rather spectacular claim: Paolo Sarpi, the most holy friar of Venice, secretly did not believe in God, and was in fact Europe's first atheist in the modern sense of the word.

The greatest mind of his age AND the first atheist? It is a story seemingly too romantic to be true, and it was taken that way by most Venetian scholars when Wootton published his book. They claimed that, though radically anti-papal, and a regular correspondent of the most heretical thinkers of his time, nonetheless he was a thoroughgoing, faith-based Christian of the Early-church Fathers variety.

So, which is it, Unconventional Christian or Secret Atheist?

His life was divided into three stages: that of the Theological Prodigy, the Scientist-Scholar, and the Statesman. His gift for scholarship and debate was recognized early. He possessed a photographic memory paired with an uncompromising sense of intellectual rigor that brooked no theological frippery. As a teenager, he entered the Servite order of friars, and soon became their intellectual superstar, paraded at public disputations as an unconquerable prodigy. He gained a reputation for unequalled canonical and historical insight, and was soon brought to Mantua (where Isabella d'Este had ruled but a handful of decades previously) as a court adviser, in which capacity his political advice was frequently sought and invariably sound.

Mantuan court life, however, didn't fully agree with him. It took up time that could have been devoted to study, and the Gonzaga currently ruling was prone to elaborate practical jokes. One of these involved Sarpi as an integral if unwilling player. A donkey was born, and Gonzaga had Sarpi compile all the astrological data surrounding the birth to send to the most famous astrologers of the day, who returned verdicts that the newborn would, undoubtedly, attain the rank of prince, or perhaps even pope (and, as future events would show, the Catholic Church would have come off little the worse had that donkey attained the pontificate instead of Paul V, but we'll come to that soon enough).

Quitting Mantua and returning to his life of study, he authored a series of definitive scientific treatises while at the same time ascending in responsibility in the Servite order, taking the lead in their theological battles against the scheming Jesuits. His scientific work included fundamental insights into optics, anatomy, magnetism, mathematics, astronomy, metallurgy, and engineering. In fact, his reputation in this last field was so great that inventors from all over Europe would bring him their devices for evaluation. Without being told, he could discern at a glance what the proposed device was for, and how it might be mechanically improved.

A genius, surely, and a man of unrivalled renown for personal piety, but was there a great secret beneath the mask of doctrinal conformity? For it was around the time of his early scientific work that he jotted down the private notes that have come to us as the *Pensieri*, and which Wootton used as the basis for his claim of Sarpi's fundamental atheism. In these notes, Sarpi took the observations of Averroes as to the practical crowd-control nature of religion, and Pietro Pomponazzi on the non-existence of personal immortality several steps further.

Not only is the soul not immortal, and most religions the product of societal conditioning, but God himself is little more than a social construct built out of the psychological vices of men. Sarpi sees humans as yearning intemperately after the impossible, mourning the limitations on their power and lifespan, and assuaging those limitations in fantasies of absolute power, in deity-crafting. This, Sarpi explains, is the real reason behind the inconsistency of even our most carefully crafted gods, why they are presented as simultaneously Beyond Emotion and Ragingly Jealous, as Unchanging but somehow Touched By Prayer. The incoherency of our gods is the trail of our own warring fantastical appetites—they don't make sense because we, as a mass, don't tend to make sense.

At best, then, religion is a "medicine" to be administered to those too sick to deal

of *faith.* Sarpi's extensive work as a commentator and defender of religion, and his exemplary and humble life as a friar do indeed make for a potent counterbalance to the *Pensieri,* but their role is, I think, somewhat weakened by the fact that Sarpi wrote *an entire text* on how to act one way while believing something entirely separate.

Whether an atheist or not, the last phase of Sarpi's career dealt such a fundamental blow to one of Catholicism's most potent weapons that on its strength alone, Sarpi deserves the thanks of humanity in general and humanists in particular. For the pope had grown hungry to undo the historical independence of the Venetian Republic, and chose as his entry point the property laws of Venice. The church had, through bequeathals, become the major landowner in Venetia, never surrendering property once acquired, and since that church land was untaxed, the end result was that the church got richer while the remaining landowners and workers bore ever higher tax burdens. Sensibly, Venice passed a law that forbid the church to hold any more bequeathed territory. This hit the papal pocketbook, and the pope responded in a fury in 1606, imposing interdiction and excommunication on all of Venetia until the law was reversed.

At this moment, Venice turned to Paolo Sarpi. Seven times, Venice had been interdicted, and every time it had folded to papal might. Understandably so—the interdict and excommunication of a territory effectively dissolved all social bonds. Sons needed not respect parents. Spouses were no longer considered married. Subjects weren't required to obey rulers. No church ceremonies could be performed, and all

with life as it is, but for those of a strong mental constitution, it is unnecessary and even harmful to their moral and intellectual development. The true philosopher, then, must seek contentment in the things of the day, pay lip service to the beliefs of the masses, and in private pursue his own moderate pleasures, realizing his finiteness

and never attempting to push beyond his natural, material boundaries.

In spite of the striking originality and daring of these ideas, there are those who consider them either thought experiments, not seriously meant, or notions that reflect on the role of *reason* in religion which do not touch Sarpi's supposed vaunting residents were declared beyond the grace of Christ. It was a big deal, and when the pope used these weapons, he nearly always got his way.

But then, the pope had never faced a man like Sarpi. Sarpi's advice was bold and simple—to carry on the business of state and society as if nothing had happened. In effect, to ignore the papal interdiction completely, and to compel any priests who complied with it to re-open their churches and continue their work under the threat of legal punishment. The nation, which the pope expected to be awash in chaos and revolution, effectively returned to its business, suffering no obvious harm from this, the pope's greatest weapon.

Pope Paul V was livid. It was bad enough that all of Venetia was ignoring his sacred condemnation, but their cause was becoming that of Europe, the papacy itself looking more ridiculous with each passing day that the excommunication and interdiction did precisely nothing to alter the prosperous course of Venetian life. Weeks passed, and the pope's cause was abandoned by all but, of course, Spain. When reconciliation was finally effected, it was entirely to Venice's credit, the pope lifting

his Dread Weapons while Venice offered effectively nothing in return, admitting of no wrong, and changing no law. Sarpi's bold move had effectively destroyed the pope's greatest secular threat. It would never be used against a sovereign territory again.

The pope and Venice had been reconciled, if begrudgingly, leaving Paul V to work out his frustration on ever more bloody plans to do away with his nemesis, Paolo Sarpi. When attempts to bribe the officials of Venice into surrendering Sarpi to the pope failed, he hired gangs of assassins to permanently solve the Sarpi problem. The first group was apprehended, but a second squad of five men succeeded in accosting Sarpi on the way to his monastery, stabbing him twice in the neck, and one final time through the temple, the blade emerging through his cheek and lodging in the bone of his skull.

But a simple stiletto *through the skull* wasn't enough to take Fra Paolo down. Within weeks, he was back on the streets, his scars a source of pride to Venetians who considered him the walking instantiation of their invulnerability. Though the pope wouldn't stop sending hit squads to Venice, all of those that followed were

discovered and dealt with long before they threatened Venice's favorite citizen.

For the rest of his life, Sarpi produced a steady stream of political tracts dealing with the secular usurpation of power by the religious authorities, railing against the legal immunity of priests, the use of criminals and prostitutes to line the church coffers, and, in his greatest and most famous work, the *History of the Council of Trent*, he crafted a timeless and detailed exposé of the shady papal vote-packing that turned Catholicism sharply away from its one chance at honest and significant internal reform.

Sarpi died quietly and peacefully in 1623 after an extended bout of fever, dictating sage political advice to the very end. His replacements at the helm of Venetian statesmanship lacked both his courage and imagination, and within a year, the once fiercely independent nation was scrambling pathetically for the pope's favor, even neglecting to erect a nameplate over Sarpi's grave, lest the act incur the papal wrath. Sarpi was finally publicly recognized with a statue in his honor erected in 1892, a late but poignant thanks from the city he loved, honored, and protected to the last.

FURTHER READING

There are two essential books in English for grasping the significance and complexity of Sarpi's life and thought. The first, *Fra Paolo Sarpi: Greatest of the Venetians*, was written by Alexander Robinson in 1894 and, though something of an unrestrained rave, in Sarpi's case the hyperbole is warranted. For him, Sarpi is the ultimate combination of modesty and brilliance, resolution and humanity, one of history's few nearly perfect people, whose Christianity ran deep in an era of religious superficiality and profiteering. A century later, David Wootton's *Paolo Sarpi: Between Renaissance and Enlightenment* (1983), attempted to rewrite everything we thought we knew about Sarpi, and via an analysis of the *Pensieri* and a study of Sarpi's intellectual influences, largely succeeds. Robinson's is by far the superior book in terms of style and depth, but contains nothing of Sarpi's radical philosophy, so if that's your primary interest, flagging down a used copy of Wootton is pretty much your only option.

Reason Strikes Back: Baruch Spinoza, the Most Dangerous Man in Europe

By 1670, all of the pieces of modern humanism were in place, waiting for one guiding intellect to join them together at last for a complete assault on the ramparts of organized religion. Abelard had cast doubt on the consistency of the church fathers, Averroes and Albertus Magnus had attacked the cult of theological authority, Pietro Pomponazzi had dismantled the immortal soul, Paolo Sarpi had defanged the temporal authority of the church, and Thomas Hobbes had advocated for a vigorous materialism that rewrote the meaning of good, evil, heaven, and hell. Each had a profound impact on the reordering of some aspect of Europe's religious life, but one man was feared as the greatest threat to the very foundation of religion itself since the dawn of recorded history: Baruch Spinoza (1632-1677), the architect of atheism.

Unlike Hobbes, who hadn't achieved anything of note during the first four decades of his life, Spinoza was, from the first, That Kid. The one who not only had all the answers in class, but could build on the facts with a dizzying natural ability, reaching conclusions that left his classmates reeling and his teacher, rabbi Saul Morteira, beaming in the hope that here, at last, was a student worthy of him. Like most teachers with gifted students, he assumed that Spinoza's intelligence would cause him to become a miniature version of himself, and didn't seem to consider for a moment that something deeper was at work beneath the outward signs of respect and consideration.

Supremely confident in the persuasiveness of his own scriptural interpretations, Morteira fed the young student as much Hebrew, history, and commentary as he could, not noticing when Spinoza's sharp

but subtle questions revealed a curiosity that was working quietly against the weight of Hebrew tradition. And perhaps Spinoza himself didn't realize the dangerous implications of his speculations until he became the student of Franciscus van den Enden, one of the strangest figures in the history of Dutch radicalism. Van den Enden was to be Spinoza's Latin teacher, but as a thorough-going critic of religion, advocate of gender and racial equality, and part-time political revolutionary looking to establish a democratic state in Normandy, he ultimately offered the bookish adolescent something far more subversive than ablative absolute constructions.

Van den Enden was part of a growing subculture of religious skeptics who flourished in the open liberality of the Dutch Republic's golden age. A small nation which resisted the military might of both Habsburg Spain and Bourbon France at their respective heights, and which challenged English commercial supremacy, all while operating a model government based on religious toleration and political openness, the Dutch Republic was, for half a century, the epicenter of radical thought in Europe. The Jewish Spinoza family had come there seeking refuge from the irregular genocide practiced by the Habsburgs, and for his whole life Baruch Spinoza would know a degree of comfort and intellectual freedom that would have been impossible in any other European land of the time.

His doubts about the veracity of the Old Testament encouraged by van den Enden, and his father's trading business facing bankruptcy at the hands of British piracy, Spinoza began distancing himself from the Jewish community of Amsterdam. He

stopped attending religious services and spoke in private of his new ideas concerning the nature of God, the priesthood, miracles, and Nature. Word was not long in reaching the community elders, who begged him to recant, to return to the fold and reclaim the status of Honored Son he had known in youth. Instead, Spinoza railed against his accusers, all but daring them to excommunicate them.

Which they promptly did, on July 27, 1656. As a Jew, Spinoza was on the margins of European society. As an excommunicate Jew, he was at the margins of those margins, the absolute outsider whose ejection from the embrace of all tradition only made him a sharper observer thereof. For the rest of his life, Spinoza lived modestly, supporting himself as a lens-grinder while eating only the simplest of foods, living in a series of rented rooms, and dressing in plain, durable clothes. He thought about philosophy and God, chatted with his landlords, and diligently ground lenses, filling the air with the glass powder that lacerated lungs already weak by nature, contributing to his premature death.

The remaining twenty-one years of his life established Spinoza as the Most Dangerous Man in Europe, read secretly everywhere in spite of the official prohibition of his few texts. The most explosive of those published in his lifetime was the *Tractatus Theologico-Politicus* of 1670, a tract which portrayed God as the immanent cause of the natural world, and nothing more. Employing his training as a Hebraist, Spinoza pointed out the startling coincidence between biblical authors and the ideas about God and Law that they put forth. Undertaking an extensive investigation of the motivations of each author, he shows that what generations have taken to be the deep truths of scripture are really just the result of various authorial perspectives, and often ignorant ones at that. Not understanding Nature, and desiring the universe to be shaped according to their own personal makeups, they called ordinary events miraculous and ventured absurd and self-serving notions of how God works in the universe.

Pressing the point further, in the notorious Chapter VI, Spinoza argued against the reality of miracles, stating that they were either ordinary events viewed by people unschooled in the workings of Nature or fits of imagination bleeding over into reality. The God of Spinoza does not act in the world, does not have emotions, does not support one people over another, does not wish for things, and does not ask for worship. He is, rather, the substance which underlies the universe, a completely indifferent source of natural law to whom prayers and sacrifice are nothing whatsoever.

This view of God, one who could not be bribed or pleased, and who offered neither punishment nor advice, was a trident in the heart of standard theology. While theologians argued over aspects of God, and definitions of good and evil, Spinoza offered the sober reality that, if even the authors of the Bible couldn't clear away their local historical prejudices in interpreting God's nature, a man coming thousands of years later, with an incomplete knowledge of the base languages involved, and a totally different historical context, had no chance of saying anything except the pre-existing content of his own religious fancy. Good and evil are just what we call things that are useful and appealing to us or not, but Nature makes no

such distinction. Tragedy is inflicted upon the innocent as often as triumph is meted out to the villainous, all following rigidly mechanical laws emanating from the structure of the universe, and there's nothing to be done about any of it.

He would expand these ideas in his posthumous masterwork, the *Ethics,* which had to be smuggled out of his house in an unmarked crate lest it fall into the wrong hands and be destroyed in manuscript. It is a towering work which attempted to display Spinoza's complete system with geometric precision, the philosophical counterpart of Euclid's *Elements.* It was his final statement of belief, and if written in a more sober tone than the *Tractatus,* was even more radical in its content. Since God is essentially just a *nom de guerre* for Nature, and Nature is governed entirely by mechanistic cause and effect, there can be no such thing as free will in any meaningful sense. Rather, there are just people, striving to actualize their personal natures to the fullest extent possible, and forming societies to do so.

When such people come across something that meets their needs, they have a natural tendency to think it was made specifically for them, and so craft notions of Providence from crude matter. When they are foiled in their ambitions, they seek an outer source to propitiate, and thus are born superstition and the power of priests. Spinoza exhorts us to turn away from anything that demands the sacrifice of our reason, or the freedom to investigate the workings of Nature. Any government or church which claims power over minds or knowledge of God's thoughts is unworthy of its authority. Each person must employ the full power of

his reason to understand his nature, work against self-defeating desires, and pursue the needs of his particular self in joint purpose with his fellow man. Because the universe is fully determined, and our actions in it also, there is no need to feel envy for those who happen to have done better, nor to feel superior to those who have had a rougher lot in life.

Instead, we are to approach other humans with compassion and understanding, realizing that their conception of good might not be our own, and that there is no way to judge one person's path as objectively better than another's. In a Europe still finding its feet after the destruction wrought by the Thirty Years' War, Spinoza's call to relinquish self-satisfied superiority in favor of a broad-based sympathy was strikingly original, and formed the positive ethical core of modern humanism. By combining scriptural critique with an uncompromising materialism, and welding both of those onto a new secular ethics of inclusivity, Spinoza produced the foundation of not only the Enlightenment, but the basic vocabulary of present humanism.

Throughout his life, Spinoza's motto was Caution. He kept the sensibilities of his Christian audience in mind, seeking to wean them of their dependence on Jesus Christ by degrees, focusing on the Old Testament and letting the implications trickle through to the New. For all his caution, however, the consequences of his philosophy were plain to all, and Spinoza watched friend after friend turn vehemently upon him, upbraiding him for his arrogance

in supposing that he, and he alone, knew better than thousands of years of religious experts. He was called the most vile, foul, and dangerous human being in the history of religion. His friends, the Koerbagh brothers, were put on trial for espousing atheistic doctrines. Van den Enden traveled to France to foment his beloved Normandy rebellion and was hung for his troubles. Leibniz, the greatest mind in Europe, eagerly sought him out in private, and condemned him vehemently in public.

And yet, his life went on, supported by a handful of true friends and a growing army of those attracted to his views, but too afraid to be seen publicly defending him. He was never arrested, never driven from his home country, and in fact lived, to all appearances, precisely the life he desired, a simple life of the mind. When he died, it was suddenly, without warning, though his health had always been precarious. Within a year, his *Ethics* was published, along with some of the secret correspondence that had flown between his humble rented rooms and the rest of Europe. Spinozism became synonymous with atheism, and his philosophical system proved fresh for generations of intellectual outsiders. His comments about the consequences of linguistic degradation for religious exegesis found their way into Herder's revolutionary linguistic theory, while his observations about humans crafting gods in their own image inspired Feuerbach's dialectic critique of Christianity. From being the outcast's outcast, he has become the philosopher's philosopher.

FURTHER READING

Spinoza is now very much in style again, and there is no shortage of academic works seeking to ride the modish wave while it lasts. For those interested more in what Spinoza actually thought and less in what some opportunistic comp lit department associate professor hopes desperately will turn into a tenure-securing book, there are some neat options out there. Matthew Stewart's *The Courtier and the Heretic* is a dual biography of Spinoza and Leibniz that is that rarest of things, an academically responsible book that at the same time has an ear for elegant prose. More imposingly, Jonathan Israel's *Radical Enlightenment: Philosophy and the Making of Modernity: 1650-1750*, is a titan of a text with a set of wonderful chapters on Spinoza and the Dutch radical philosophers at its core. If you want to read some original Spinoza, the *Tractatus* makes for a much more digestible start than the *Ethics,* and is widely available, and there's an inexpensive Dover volume that includes selections from his intense correspondence which is quite fun.

Thomas Hobbes:
Atheist. Materialist. Radical?

The two mainstays of American high school history education are over-selling Napoleon III and lying about Thomas Hobbes. Every year, a new crop of students is informed that Hobbes was a bitter, reactionary conservative who believed that life is nasty, brutish, and short and that we should all live under a Divine Right absolutist monarch. They are then told to write an essay Comparing and Contrasting John Locke and Thomas Hobbes, with Hobbes as the Snidely Whiplash to Locke's virtuous, freedom-loving Dudley Do Right.

In reality, Thomas Hobbes (1588-1679) was perhaps the most daring and thorough-going materialist since Lucretius, with ideas about psychology and motivation that we've only caught up to in the neuroscience boom of the past few decades. Hobbes held that everything was corporeal, and all events the result of the motions of particles. The idea of a Cartesian dualism between body and soul struck him as clearly false, and he set out to demonstrate how all of our sense data are the result of the transference of motion from outside stimuli to our internal organs. The world rewrites our physical organism through stimulus bombardment, and all memory and imagination result from the physical accessing of these chemically stored sensations. Our thoughts are the result of the motion of physical entities, like everything else.

Starting from that premise, Hobbes ended up some rather spectacular places. Whereas most writers of the era took reason as the fundamental property of humanity, Hobbes saw it as an appetitive ordering force. We are driven forward on the legs of our desires, appetites, and fears, and it is the job of the reason to evaluate and weigh the content of our various desire streams.

Reason is the process of ordering and ranking desires, a definition of neural decision making algorithms three centuries before its time.

Impressive enough, but it goes deeper. Because everything about our mental life is the result of motions and observations impressed on our organism from without, Hobbes concluded that the idea of an absolute state of ultimate happiness was psychologically naïve. Happiness is not something you achieve, it is a social and comparative construct that must constantly find new ends if it is to last. Our emotional states are based on a constant monitoring of the success and failure of those around us. Envy and anger, joy and laughter, are all founded on an evaluation of how we are running the race of life relative to other people we know. There is no absolute good way of living, only a thousand daily acts of comparison and adjustment. This view, which was held for centuries to be a far too cynical notion of mankind, is in the Internet Age receiving its first real experimental treatment. Every study that is released about Facebook Depression—the phenomenon of feeling depressed not because of bad events that are happening to you, but because of the ceaseless inundation of other people's good status posts, is a stirring affirmation of Hobbes's socially relativist emotional insight.

Now, because happiness is relative and largely competitive, that means that, left to our own devices, life becomes about an unchecked grab for the means of securing a greater share of happiness than those around us. Which gets super nasty, super fast. The state of nature for Hobbes is a place where nobody is safe, a realm of absolute equality (for Hobbes believed in the total equality of all men, which got

him into not a little trouble with his noble patrons—even his beloved absolute monarch is just a dude like everybody else, who happens to be installed with everybody's mutually forsworn authority) where murder was an effective and convenient means of getting what one wanted. You don't need to be strong or smart to push a guy off a cliff when he's not expecting it.

That state of nature leads into the one thing everybody thinks they know about Hobbes: his position on absolute government. And yes, it's entirely true that he thought the only way to guarantee the safety of all individuals was to erect a central authority who had in his hands all of the legislative and executive power that humans could surrender to him. He preferred that authority to be a monarch, but didn't leave out the possibility that it might be something else. The important thing was that, in this system, nobody, and no group no matter the size, had any natural right to dominance over anybody else. And again, I think, it was ahead of its time.

People became so afraid of Hobbes's vision of society that they responded with a The Majority Is Always Right approach to government which allowed minorities to get regularly ground to dust for the convenience of the majority. The idea that the job of government is to protect the minority from the majority by using its authority to override their massed power is the essence of the Civil Rights state, and is something present within the Hobbesian theory, but not in the diffuse democratic theories that dominated the eighteenth and nineteenth century American discourses. I don't mean to say that Hobbes was a proto-minority-rights-enthusiast in the modern sense—he clearly had monarchs primarily in mind,

and said that our obedience is to them no matter how terrible they are, because the alternative was worse—but I will say that his concern with erecting a system powerful enough to protect the most vulnerable from the most rapacious whims of the majority is one that has interesting resonances with what we've come to view as government's social role.

Materialist, clearly. Political visionary—if you squint a bit, I think so. But atheist? Surely not. Yes, he was accused of atheism on many occasions, but everybody who writes anything about religion is accused of being an atheist by somebody eventually. Yet Hobbes's writings on religion *were* unique in their uncompromising application of materialism and causality, and if not atheistic in the limited sense of Denying the Existence of God, were certainly anti-theistic in the sense of Denying the Ability of Religion to Say Meaningful Things.

As to God, Hobbes held that, if there was a beginning of the universe, then God is the name you have to give to what started it. Beyond that, you can't say anything use-ful or descriptive. He had no patience with the endless theorizing of Scholasticism, or with attempts to establish ideas upon the-ological authority. What we take to be de-scriptions of God, he was among the first to point out, are really only honorifics. In a move that Feuerbach would extend to its fullest implications two centuries later, he insisted on rigorously examining the divine so-called attributes and finding their source in ourselves. A peripheral member of the Great Tew Circle, he recognized that what one authority held irrevocably true, a dozen deemed indubitably false, and that to seek unity from that hornet's nest of opinion was to court futility.

If the universe had a beginning, and it might not have, it was because of God, and if God exists, then he must be a corporeal being, because nothing incorporeal exists. That's about all that Hobbes is willing to as-sert as to the content of religion. Regarding religion's temporal power, it must be en-tirely subservient to the monarch. Because religious doctrine is arbitrary and human, Hobbes infers, it doesn't matter which one the monarch chooses for his people. Once the monarch picks, the people are com-pelled to follow all the outward norms of that religion, but are free to believe what-ever they want privately. In some places, he declares that a monarch can't pick a religion that denies the divinity of Jesus, though that seems more of a concession to environment rather than a result of his basic theoretical structure.

For striking at the temporal power of religion, for branding superstition some-what ironically as irrational fears that don't happen to be officially sanctioned, and doubting the basic utility of religious state-ments, Hobbes was branded an atheist and had to spend much ingenuity warding off the imputation, one of many hurled at him by an age that couldn't yet understand what he was trying to do. His ninety-two years of life were unlike that of any figure we've looked at so far. Had he died at the age of fifty, he would be almost totally unremembered by history. The first decades of his life he spent as a tutor to William Cavendish's son, William Cavendish, and after that to his grandson, William Cavendish. He went with his charges on the grand tours of Europe, translated Thucydides, wrote some unremarkable essays about Rome, and generally killed time as a typical, if bright, servant in a glorious household.

Then came the Civil War, the beheading of the English king Charles I in 1649, and the years of Cromwell's Protectorate. Hobbes fled to Europe before things could get too tight for a confirmed Royalist like himself, and while there he deepened his interest in the natural sciences and mathematics while watching the English tragedy play itself out. *Leviathan*, the work we know him for now, was not published until 1651, when he was already sixty-three years old, an inspiring fact for anybody who is under sixty-three and has yet to accomplish anything in particular. It was a more subtle reworking of points he had made in 1640's *Elements of Law, Natural and Political*, and contained the full working out of his psychological, religious, and political beliefs, and how they all resulted in the need for a mutual transfer of power from glory-chasing individuals to a central authority. Hobbes would continue writing on these themes for the rest of his life, along with observations about the state of English universities, European science and, most unfortunately, outlandish mathematical claims to have squared the circle. Ridiculed for his mathematical pretenses, reviled for his theological skepticism, and taken to task for his relativistic stance on the existence of good and evil and his cynical view of human pleasure, the last decades of his life were spent in an almost constant state of defense.

And perhaps that was inevitable. How could an average seventeenth-century scholar know that memory and imagination are physical events, that decision making is the result of internal appetitive evaluations, that good and evil are just terms people give to things they like and dislike as they seek that small bit of satisfaction that comes when you are a fraction of a nose ahead of your fellow runners in life's race, or that the loose rhetoric of the Popular Will would result in as much oppression of the minority as liberty for the majority? To see all of that in the middle of the seventeenth century would take a person devoted to the methods and assumptions of natural science, and possessed of the mental fortitude to see them through to even their most depressing and unfashionable ends.

It would take a Thomas Hobbes, and unfortunately for him, there was only one of those around.

FURTHER READING

Hobbes scholars are, perhaps necessarily, an odd lot. It takes a bit of screwiness to look at the author of *Leviathan* and say, I'm going to make that guy my life's work. But that very oddness also makes Hobbes books generally amongst the most fun to read for seventeenth-century philosophy. I'd start with *Hobbes* (1905) by Sir Leslie Stephen—it was the last book he wrote, and is a nice, brisk introduction to the many curious corners of Hobbes's thought. Once you've read that, if you want to go into some more depth, A.P. Martinich's *Hobbes: A Biography* (1999) is another great, fun book, which has the advantage of having been written after neuroscience began adding weight to many Hobbesian ideas that had been discarded as too mechanistic and dour for consideration. Then, when your kids come to you to ask for help on writing their Hobbes-Locke paper, you can tell them, "This is what you're going to say... Thomas Hobbes was a f***ing rock star."

We're All Mad Here: The Seventeenth-Century Tolerance of Pierre Bayle

B ehold the Truth" is a sentence of omen, perched at the tense verge of bloodshed. It demands conformity, throws up resistance to intellectual exchange and, when frustrated, is often quite fine with sending out sword-wielding burly men to enforce its claims. And yet, for a millennium and a half, philosophers and Christians, Platonists and skeptics, agreed on nothing save that The Truth was the goal of all inquiry. Even Descartes, whose program was to be one of universal doubt, ended with a laundry list of established and undeniable metaphysical truths. Amidst all of that strident, continent-wide self-assuredness, it took moxy unto foolhardiness to stand up and say, "Eh. People think a lot of things. Best to just let them live and prosper as best they can, be they atheist or Jew or Christian." But that's precisely what a sickly book nerd named Pierre Bayle (1647-1706) did from within the depths of unspeakable religious oppression.

Bayle's list of philosophic Firsts runs almost as long as that of the number of first-rank philosophers he influenced. Both the French Enlightenment and English Deism rest on the shoulders of his broad-minded and encyclopedic work. He was the first European thinker to eschew system-building as the *stuff* of philosophy. Having watched Descartes and Spinoza begin so promisingly, only to lose themselves in the building of top-heavy and totally unprovable assertions about the nature of divinity, Bayle argued persuasively that all such projects are intellectually doomed.

He was also the first to argue that a society of atheists would, morally, operate pretty much the same as any other society since morality comes from our shared humanity, not our particular religious beliefs. He also

lowered the continental dread of atheists by pointing out that they are, essentially, geeky bookworms too busy with hunting down obscure theological references to engage in the bloodshed and debauchery that they were generally believed to revel in. During a time when slightly different shades of Christianity were falling over themselves to slaughter each other, he argued passionately for a tolerance that extended to all, *including* the Muslim, *including* the Jew, and *including* the nonbeliever.

As you might imagine, his life was never easy. Born just one year shy of the end of the Europe-breaking Thirty Years' War, in which a third of the population died trying to enforce various religious orthodoxies, he grew up the chronically ill son of a Protestant minister. His refuge was books, to the detriment of his fragile health. When he was first sent to the Protestant Academy of Puylaurens to study, he worked so hard, ignoring vacations and meals and all amusements, that he wrecked his body and had to return home to recover. Having learned everything Puylaurens could teach him, his father sent him to the Jesuit college in Toulouse, which featured the most rigorous courses in logic in the country.

The Protestant father expected a bit of argumentative gloss for his son, nothing more. You can well imagine his surprise, then, when in 1669 that son converted to Catholicism, persuaded by the deceptively solid arguments of his professors. He needn't have worried, though. That rush of initial enthusiasm was dashed quickly on the accumulated absurdities of Catholic dogma. The host of miracles and saints, the details of transubstantiation—these were not the stuff of long-term belief for a mind as honed and deeply read as Bayle's. A year later, he abjured his conversion, and fled to Geneva.

Why did he have to flee? Well, whereas French law was at the time somewhat tolerant of Protestants, it was vigorously antagonistic to people who converted to Catholicism, and then fell back out of it. Intellectual recidivists were dangerous examples of the tenuousness of Catholic belief, standing embarrassments to the nation's One True religion, and had to be ruthlessly oppressed lest they touch off a surge of de-conversion. Geneva was a sanctuary for exiled Calvinists, stuffed with dour but brilliant academics who sharpened Bayle's critical sense.

But Bayle was a Frenchman, and needed to be in France. So, he changed his name (to Bèle in an act of subterfuge that represented the true *bare minimum* of effort) and took up a position at the Protestant Academy of Sedan in 1675. He stayed there for six years, until Louis XIV decided he'd had enough of the whole Idea of Protestant academies, and suppressed the lot in 1681. Bayle had to flee again, this time to Rotterdam, where he remained until his death, watching from the sidelines as France plunged into a self-crippling wave of religious fervor on the heels of Louis's 1685 revocation of the Edict of Nantes, undoing at a stroke Henry IV's hard-won toleration for France's Protestants.

From the bracing intellectual liberty of Rotterdam, Bayle composed the works that made his name and inaugurated the anti-metaphysical skepticism that inspired an intellectual epoch and whose program we largely still follow today. His first salvo was the *Various Thoughts on the Comet of 1680,* a *tour de force* in which he railed not only against the various superstitious imbecilities that had accompanied the appearance of a startling comet in the European sky, but made a host of arguments totally unheard of in Western philosophy. It was in this pamphlet that he painted atheists as moral and philosophically engaged, and hazarded the hypothesis that an atheist society would be ethically and morally just as good as a God-fearing one, if not better. He surveyed the diversity of religious opinions and placed them against the relative uniformity of human passions to move towards a humans-first account of morality, going so far as to say that a society which relied solely on religion for its sense of morality would fall apart in unchecked licentiousness and bloodshed within weeks.

He portrayed religion as the lagging edge of human development, a body of ideas always huffing to catch up with the positive inclusivity of humanity's evolution. Society finds ways to advance and improve itself, the individuals within that society take those principles eventually as their personal core values, and then, after much resistance and growling, religion takes up those same principles, rewrites its dogmas, and attempts to pretend that it's *always* had those views. It's an amusing portrayal of Christianity's Orwellian relation to its past that rings just as true now as it did in 1682.

That same year saw the publication of the *General Critique of Father Maimbourg's History of Calvinism*, a resounding call for universal toleration that was, of course, burned in Paris for daring to suggest that uniformity of belief wasn't worth the constant and bloody civil war it would take to create it. Two years later, on the eve of the revocation of Nantes, he had a go at Descartes, and at all philosophy which claimed to have found universal truths. Using the two-pronged attack of his Jesuit training in logic and his massive acquaintance with world philosophy, he showed the gradations by which personal opinion shaded into absolute dogma, and how the manifold nature of the former manifested in the tendentiousness of the latter. Lots of people think lots of things and come up with lots of systems to justify those lots of thoughts, and the very diversity of those accounts should give a reasonable person pause when considering any single claim to universal truth. Philosophy is religion is superstition is opinion sanctified by the passage of time. All that some three *centuries* before Derrida, mind you.

At this point, the Catholics hated him for taking to account their carnage-soaked mania for conversion and expansion, but Bayle could still have made for himself a nice home as a Calvinist hero, if he were interested in wealth and comfort. He was not. The intolerance of the Catholics, he felt, was matched by that of the Protestants, who were just as zealous in their execration of nonbelievers (even those of just slightly different belief) as the Catholics. He lashed out on all sides at those who would use the arm of government to force all men to believe the same. He lost his governmental pension, which made little difference to a man who lived as simply as did Bayle. His personal frugality and modest living impressed even his fiercest enemies, and there would be plenty of those in the years to come.

In 1684, he launched a book review periodical which presented to a European-wide audience the variety of the freethinking literature being produced by the exciting open presses of the Dutch Republic. It was a runaway success, the essential reading for anybody who wanted to keep up with the latest intellectual developments, as filtered through Bayle's encyclopedic grasp of history, philosophy, and literature. From that triumph, Bayle launched the *Historical and Critical Dictionary* in 1695, the work we know him for today. It was a massive catalogue of humanity's myths, thoughts, and foibles, recounted by a master of deep criticism. From Mahomet to the Virgin Mary to the multiplication of saints to John Calvin to the brutal heroes of the Bible, Bayle let the full content of his amassed wisdom flow in the pages of the *Dictionary*, directed by his overriding principles of toleration and universal skepticism. It was the intellectual ancestor of the *Encyclopedia* of Diderot and the *Devil's Dictionary* of Ambrose Bierce, and is simultaneously profound, amusing, and ever fresh.

Between the critical and popular successes of his book review and the *Dictionary*, Bayle had made himself a name as the equitable and trustworthy arbiter of European thought. Foreign courts vied to make him their resident philosopher, but the man who flourished in the intellectual freedom of Rotterdam couldn't be budged by promise of money or fame. He continued to write, facing down the wrath of Catholic and Calvinist alike as his body, never over-reliable, slowly betrayed him. He died in 1706 after a long illness, and was buried in the free Dutch soil of Rotterdam.

FURTHER READING

Much of Bayle's work has been translated into English, and his work on the comet of 1680 makes for a good introduction to the breadth and originality of his thought. If you read French, there's a book that combines a passionately told overview of his life with a nice selection of excerpts from *Comet*, the *Dictionary*, his book reviews, and letters: *Pierre Bayle: Sa Vie, Ses Idees, Son Influence, Son Œuvre* by Albert Cazes (1905) and available as a University of Michigan reprint.

Novelist. Journalist. Spy. Wit and Sexual Liberation in Seventeenth-Century England.

LONDON, 1677.

APHRA! I'M...

A TIME TRAVELLER. I KNOW. I NEED YOU TO DELIVER THIS LETTER TO MY LITERARY DESCENDANTS.

A QUEST? EXCELLENT! WHAT'S THE NOTE SAY?

IT'S AN APPEAL TO CONTINUE MY WORK, TO SHOW THE PUBLIC THE EQUAL WORTH OF MEN'S *AND WOMEN'S* FULL FREEDOM OF SEXUAL CHOICE, HOW EROTIC LOVE CAN ENHANCE OUR LIVES IF WE LIFT THE RELIGIOUS MYSTICISM FROM IT!

LONDON, 1720.

HOW TRULY SHE WRITES! IMAGINE, A WORLD WHERE WE COULD LOVE WHEN AND WHO WE WOULD!

FREE FROM ARTIFICIAL CODES OF SOCIAL CONDUCT AND EXPECTATION.

GREAT! SO YOU'RE BOTH ON BOARD?

DELARIVIER MANLEY!

STILL JUST DAVE!

ELIZA HAYWOOD!

NOT REMOTELY! I LOVE APHRA, BUT IF YOU TAKE OUT ALL THE PLEASURE SHAMING, MY NEW ATALANTIS WOULD BE LIKE HALF A CHAPTER LONG!

AND I KIND OF HAD MY HEART SET ON REPLACING ARTIFICIAL *SOCIAL* CODES WITH ARTIFICIAL CODES SPRUNG FROM ROMANTICIZED *IDEALISM*...

SURE, BECAUSE WHY HAVE ONE CENTURY OF VICTORIANISM WHEN YOU COULD HAVE *TWO?*

There was a time, after the passing of Catholic supremacy and before Romanticism shaded into the idealized half-century-long fainting spell of Victorianism, when it looked like women were at last gaining for themselves a place at civilization's table. Christina was monarch in Sweden, Sophia Charlotte of Hannover was directing the continent's philosophical life, Maria Merian was conducting entomological expeditions to the jungles of Surinam, and in England, a trio later known as the Fair Triumvirate of Wit were playing a complicated role in the arena of public discourse that would not be available to women for another two centuries.

Aphra Behn (1640?-1689), Delarivier Manley (1663?-1724), and Eliza Haywood (1693?-1756) were, singly, forces of astounding ability and intricate motivation. As a whole, they represented a sustained challenge to male political, literary, and sexual supremacy that was not only intellectually forceful, but wildly popular. Three women, in three generations, each building on the work of her intellectual ancestors to produce an ultimate picture of independent and pleasurable womanhood.

As you might have guessed from the flurry of question marks in the life dates of the Triumvirate, much of their biography is lost to time. Because they were women, because records were hazily kept, and because they themselves engaged in much biographical obfuscation in their quasi-memoirs, most statements about their lives come with an appended asterisk of uncertainty. They all, however, lived highly unconventional existences. Behn was born into poverty and, to avoid debtor's prison, decided in 1666 to work as a professional spy for the British government, playing a crucial role in infiltrating the Dutch Republic,

work she was ultimately, and perhaps inevitably, never paid for.

So, to stave off bankruptcy, she turned to the theater, where the ban on female actors had just recently been lifted, and women were achieving some successes as playwrights as well. In 1677, she had a smash success with *The Rover,* and it's easy to see why. The play is a bawdy, over-the-top farce crafted in the brightest and broadest colors. The central character, a drifting soldier named Wilmore, is a disaster-prone no-account, almost genetically incapable of fidelity, who always tries to do right by his friends but whose idea of Helping always manages to ruin their lives. He is a scoundrel, and in a Proper play he would be caught in his scoundreliness, rejected by all virtuous company, and drubbed from society.

But Aphra Behn does not write Proper plays, she writes human plays, where people gleefully jettison societal codes to enjoy each other. Two females, one a courtesan and the other a soon-to-be-nun, find themselves falling in love with Wilmore, knowing full well that he's an inconstant scoundrel. But Hellena, the pre-nun, doesn't care, and is planning on a life of free inconstancy herself, to grab pleasure and dazzle and live as she can, anything to avoid the clawing monotony and libidinal insincerity of the cloister. This was the revolution of Behn's plays—they portrayed female desire in all of its colors and manifestations, without any virginal whitewashing. The females have just as much right to sexual satisfaction as the males, without shame or damage to the fundamental goodness of their character. Behn sympathetically portrays prostitutes and courtesans, and heaps not a little bit of abuse on men who clamor for virgins while allowing themselves complete sexual freedom.

Dramatic success led to a brief career in political satire, where, like her successor Delarivier Manley, she took up cudgels for the Tories against the Whigs. That might seem confusing, like if Maya Angelou hit the political circuit campaigning really energetically for Donald Trump, but there is a sense in it. Whereas the Whigs were the champions of many progressive strains in political life, the bourgeois mindset of the party in the seventeenth century was one that kept wives as chaste homemakers, while in the nobility-leaning circles of the Tories, women were granted a much more free sexual and intellectual existence. So, if you were Aphra Behn, the Tories had a surprising amount to offer. Unfortunately, she was rather *too* Tory, even for the king, and Charles II ultimately put a warrant out for her arrest when she attacked the Duke of Monmouth, Charles's illegitimate son.

She went underground until cooler heads could prevail, and ultimately abandoned political writing and returned to the farces that had made her success as a youth. She also took a few moments to write the first novel in the English language in 1688. Because, apparently, she hadn't achieved enough? Meanwhile, Delarivier Manley, her fellow Tory, was hopping from scandal to scandal. Where Behn was a playwright who had a go at political journalism, Manley was a savage political satirist who jollied around with Jonathan Swift and used her deliciously acidic pen to write devastating satires against the Duke of Marlborough and the rest of the Whig leadership.

Everything Manley did, she did audaciously. She lived in a bigamous marriage for many years, was repeatedly under threat of arrest, participated somewhat shadily in complicated *Bleak House*-esque inheritance schemes, *and* wrote purely political pamphlets that shaped public opinion and thence governmental policy. Just think about that—a woman, writing in the seventeenth century, about party politics and public policy, and accepted as the equal of Swift in those realms. Her masterwork was *The New Atalantis* (1709), in which Virtue and Justice travel a thinly disguised England looking for honorable humans, and instead finding various members of the Whig party engaged in every manner of possible debauchery and dishonesty. Unlike *The Rover*, it's a quite challenging book for a modern reader, as most of the issues and personalities described have been lost in the recesses of time and history, but for pure savage destructive political glee, it's unrivaled, and as a monument of women participating in political life, there's nothing like it until the twentieth century.

But it's hard to serve two masters. Manley wanted to show that female sexuality was a positive thing, and ought to be celebrated, but at the same time wanted to score points against the Whigs by showing them engaged in sexual excesses. Seventeenth and eighteenth-century political pamphleteering was all about lurid tales of orgies and prostitution, and Manley couldn't resist the temptation to do likewise, even as her shaming of loose women ran counter to her sympathetic portrayals of prostitutes in fiction and her own amour-filled private life.

Eliza Haywood, the last of the triumvirate, idolized Aphra Behn every bit as much as Manley, but again that idolization took an odd turn that tended to undermine Behn's literary mission. Haywood's first novel, *Love in Excess,* was a hulk of a bestseller, the most popular novel of the early eighteenth century next to *Robinson Crusoe.* Like Behn, Haywood rails at the strictures

of a society that doesn't permit women to voice their romantic preferences, and that only gives them death or the nunnery as alternatives to an arranged marriage. However, in the grand eighteenth century tradition, love undergoes an idealization in the work every bit as rigid in its boundaries as Behn's freewheeling erotic fancy was fluid.

Haywood's cult of ideal love, which makes sex a kind of secular sacrament, is very romantic and totally joyless. Haywood is as willing to heap scorn on a female character who wants sex for pure physical satisfaction as she is to pile praise and reward on a male character who nearly rapes a succession of women because he is such a *noble* slave of his ideal passion. It's a hard shift, to go from the world of Behn's flatulent and happy fornicators to Haywood's violent and demented lovers, to see open and free humanity replaced by a dangerous because abstract zeal. Commentators on Haywood point out that her heroines make choices for themselves and have definite erotic desires, but both are so circumscribed by

the author's particular notion of what does and does not count as honorable passion that the gates are rather more thrown open to Victorian sexual rarefaction than Behnian freedom.

There were but forty years between *The Rover* and *Love in Excess*, with Manley's virulent *The New Atalantis* placed firmly in the middle, and a starker tale of hero worship gone wrong you'll be hard-pressed to find. Manley, by means of wit and scorn, clawed her way impressively to an unprecedented amount of political infamy and power, and while she kept Behn's raucous Toryism, she was inconstant in its application. Haywood took passion as her watchword, pumping out sometimes three novels a year in its glorification, but put terms and conditions on it that Behn would have laughed off, yet which survived through the British Enlightenment to become the touchstone of overwrought and underhuman Romanticism.

But don't worry, any day now we'll catch up to the sexual openness and liberality of 1677. Any day now....

FURTHER READING

There's a nice edition of four of Aphra Behn's plays in the *Oxford English Drama* series edited by Jane Spencer. The notes are endnotes, which are an abomination generally, but are full of useful points on seventeenth-century linguistic usage. The two main books available for Manley are *The New Atalantis*, which is well nigh indecipherable without extensive notes, and is available in a Penguin Classics edition, and her autobiographical and delightfully self-puffing *Adventures of Rivella*, which goes into bewilderingly dense detail about the inheritance case she entangled herself in, available from Broadview Literary Texts with some nice appendices of various Manley bits.

Eliza Haywood wrote So Many Novels that most of them are still unavailable to but the hardiest of collectors. *Love in Excess* is put out by Broadview with its notes mercifully in footnote format, and if, after that, you still want more Haywood instead of re-reading Behn, which is what you SHOULD be doing, Broadview has also put out *Fantomina* and *Anti-Pamela*, her response to Samuel Richardson's massively successful innocent waif novel *Pamela* (1740).

Anthony Collins and the Bad Boys of English Deism

The United States is the country that Deism made and if the nation's founding fathers strike us as an improbable rag-tag collection of generals, writers, brewers, silversmiths, and planters, that is altogether appropriate for a revolution spawned from the ultimate misfit on the English intellectual scene. Early eighteenth-century Deism had every disadvantage conceivable, from the massive weight of the official condemnation lined up against it to the absurd personal foibles of its champions. And yet, on the strength of the few thin pamphlets produced by this group of self-sabotaging underdogs, two governments were overthrown, and over-complacent scriptural apologists found themselves for the first time in a mad scramble to defend their most basic assumptions.

The early Deists were men bound by an idea, and not much else. There was John Toland (1670-1722), a parentless vagabond not above offering his services as a spy in between scribbling radical pamphlets. Matthew Tindal (1657-1733), a pathologically punctual man who waited until his seventieth year to write the book that called into questions God's managerial skills. Thomas Chubb (1679-1747), amateur philosopher, professional candlemaker. Thomas Woolston (1668-1733), the clergyman who spent the last four years of his life in jail for blasphemy. Charles Blount (1654-1693), who shot himself after not being allowed by the state to marry his dead wife's sister. And the weightiest of them all, Anthony Collins (1676-1729), a well-off country squire and judge, friend even to his enemies, who lived a life of the utmost rectitude while writing the books that inspired Voltaire, Diderot, and Reimarus to their deadly assaults on religion and free will.

How did people so different come to devote themselves to a cause unilaterally hated? The answer, as with just about anything in English intellectual history, comes down to John Locke (1632-1704). Locke was, to put it in the modern parlance, So Over European metaphysics. To him, as to many sober British minds of the era (and since), the speculations of Descartes and his ilk appeared as unabashed examples of the Continental tendency to Make Things Up. Thinkers like Leibniz were ingenious at constructing large metaphysical systems that operated just behind the visible world, moved by the whimsical fancy of their idealistic genius and a genuine need for there to be an immaterial soul behind the machine of human existence. Inspired, intoxicated by their own visions of celestial order, they crafted certainties out of elaborate systems moored in the nothingness of abstraction, and John Locke was *not* having it.

The idea we remember Locke for, the *tabula rasa,* was one of a series of sobering punches Locke delivered to the anxious underbelly of Continental thought. The idea of pre-existing concepts placed in humanity by God so as to recognize His truth Locke demolished through a steady-on appeal to the facts of perception and the manifest materiality of thought. After Locke, building arguments for the deity on anything that smacked of Innate Ideas was to welcome ridicule. And Locke wasn't hardly done. In 1695 he produced *The Reasonableness of Christianity*, a book more significant for what it invited than what it established. This book was an honest attempt to show how reason and Christianity could walk hand in hand which fell short of its goal, but which introduced the fundamental reasonableness of Christianity as a plausible subject of debate.

John Toland took up the call the very next year in his *Christianity not Mysterious*, which he attributed to the influence of Locke and which Locke couldn't disavow fast enough. It was another in a long series of breaks which Toland resolutely did not catch. Though his book was similar to Locke's of the previous year, Locke was heralded as a defender of the faith while Toland was hounded as an atheist and infidel, and lived as a drifting tumbleweed wafting between England and the Continent for the rest of his life in search of a steady job. In retrospect, the abuse was canny, for the religious establishment saw in Toland a potential for mischief far less muted than in Locke's text. Toland was concerned with showing how the law prescribed by nature must coincide with the laws set forth by Christianity, and in effect bent the latter to fit the former and, when they wouldn't bend, pushed them subtly under the rug. He made Christianity answer to the judgment of Nature, and even if his end verdict was that, all in all, fundamental Christianity (he expressed little patience with the contradictory declarations of priest and popes) passed the test, the mere posing of the question shook something deep in the structure of Christianity's self-assuredness.

The question of Christianity's correspondence with the basic principles of human morality was posed most effectively by Matthew Tindal just three years before his death. *Christianity as Old as the Creation* (1730) had the raw nerve to point out that, if Christianity is true, it doesn't speak too well of God's planning skills. After the opening of commerce with the East and the exploration of the New World, European society was slowly coming to the realization that centuries-long cultures existed and throve without any slightest notion of a man named Jesus and his self-professed status as the son of God. China in particular seemed a land if anything more civilized in its sense of public morality and ethics than the West, boasted a culture dating back seemingly before the beginning of the world, and did it all without the personal intervention of Jehovah. If a culture can be that good without any direction from Christian dogma, Tindal dared to ask, is any of that dogma necessary? Could Christianity possibly be an expression of the fundamental laws of reason and nature if a whole major civilization needed not a jot of it?

Even if China weren't a model civilization, Tindal argued, what can we say of a God whose Very Important plan for salvation remained unheard to untold generations of families? He either doesn't care and is happy to toss them in the furnace with a "Whatcha-gonna-do?" shrug of the shoulders, or he earnestly wanted his message to reach all humanity, and was terrible at going about it. Not a good lookout either way, and the implication as Tindal saw it was that merely nationalistic gods had to go. Jehovah, a cleverly spun tribal god gone multinational, needing stripping of everything that wasn't part of the whole world's conception of divinity. Morality and law likewise. What remained after this process of descaling the divine, as Tindal reckoned, was the universal imperative to happiness. You have been given a nature to seek certain things, so seek them, and know that the act of good living is comprised of those principles so basic to humanity that you don't need them written on tablets. They are part of who you naturally are, what you naturally seek, and naturally avoid, and any

verbiage and Shalting on top of that is fruitless excess.

Tindal's master work came out in 1730 (there was a second volume, but the person to whom it was entrusted saved Christianity a further embarrassment by conveniently losing the manuscript). In between the times of Toland and Tindal strode the curious figure of Anthony Collins. What began as a polite investigation of reasonable theology in Toland became an out-and-out, single-bulb-hanging-from-a-wire-in-a-back-room interrogation of Christianity in Collins's hands. He was a trusted friend of Locke's during the great man's last years, and never ceased to express his fundamental obedience to Lockean principles even as he pushed the application of reason and questioning further than Locke would ever have contemplated. He was as puzzling, inconsistent, and sloppy as he was good-hearted and intellectually fearless. He was not a genius, nor an originator, but he could see where evidence ultimately led, and had the courage to put his conclusions before a hostile public.

His first works were nothing special. He called for an expansion of free speech and thought in England, and argued that the idea of Christian truths being Above Reason was unsound. Unfortunately in these early works, he tended to be casually incorrect in his translations, and less than rigorous in his scholarship. A self-taught book nerd of the first order (his private library was among the finest in England), he never finished college and his knowledge of classical languages was shaky. His opponents seized the opportunity to discredit him by focusing on his sloppy misappropriations rather than on the dan-

gerous content of his arguments, and he was thoroughly and utterly trounced in the marketplace of public ideas.

Understandably, Collins retired to country life thereafter, surrounding himself with his beloved books and taking upon himself the straightening of his district's shady financial situation. Thoroughly upright and hard-working, as a treasurer and a justice he won a reputation for clean dealing that protected him in the years to come from the fury that descended upon poor Toland and Woolston. He'd need it, because after a decade-long break, he returned to writing, and this time, he had his intellectual ducks in a row. In 1724 his *Discourse of the Grounds and Reasons of the Christian Religion* tore to shreds the notion that the prophecies of the Old Testament could be allegorically retrofitted to fit the needs of the New. He lampooned the eccentric attempts of Whitson to metaphorically interpret the ancient prophets to make Jesus their necessary topic, and howled in glee at Surenhusius's Baroque reordering of Hebrew words and letters to fit Christian theology. Before Collins, prophecy and miracles stood as sure testaments to the truth of Christianity. After the drubbing Collins gave Whitson, prophecy could be so no more, and all the Deists worked in concert to show the manifest uselessness of miracles as a method for conveying truth through the ages.

In the seventeenth century, English theology was sure of nothing so much as the solidity of scripture, but Collins asked questions about gradual loss of meaning and ulterior motive that would directly inspire Reimarus in his radical reinterpretation of the New Testament. The *Discourse* is important, but my favorite work by

Collins is definitely the *Philosophical Inquiry Concerning Human Liberty* of 1715. In it, Collins makes the case for a strict determinism, and for the logical meaninglessness of free will. It was the book that made a determinist of Voltaire, and which would, through the translation by arch-atheist Jacques-Andre Naigeon, impact Denis Diderot's thinking as well. In it, he puts out his theory that what we take for independent choice is actually the operation of a relatively mechanical judgment system, which assigns various values to the choices before us and picks the best. Collins's account is actually, in boldest outline, not that far from the system of decision making outlined within the last decade by neuroscientist Read Montague.

More crucially, Collins takes on issues concerning the morality of determinism. "Will we continue to have an effective conscience if we have no free will? How will justice work? Will praise and censure mean anything to us?" His answers are, as James O'Higgins has pointed out, a mixture of Bayle and Hobbes, but more approachable than the latter and more not-in-French than the former. He makes the case that you can still find happiness while thinking yourself determined, and that the lack of free will doesn't mean that people can be denied freedom from intellectual or political restraint.

England would come to forget Collins, and Deism generally. Running quietly aground in its native soil, the philosophy of freethought, religious skepticism, and political openness found a home in America and France, where Franklin and Voltaire, Paine and d'Holbach, would find in it the seed of a new way of thought, and a new nation as well. Meanwhile, in England, the arrival of Hume's absolute skepticism, boldly and rigorously stated, made the tentative and scratchy forays of the Deists seem a bit Bush League, and history, which gets nervous if it has to memorize more than one philosopher every quarter century, decided that it was best to leap from Locke straight to Hume. That makes for an easier textbook to write, but it undersells the complexity of the Enlightenment's birth. Reason did not spring fully formed from the Temple of Science, but inched its way into the sun, its tenets advanced by a collection of brave oddballs who didn't themselves realize the magnitude of the ideas they were putting forth. This was the punk youth of skepticism, the back-alley philosophizing that preceded freethought's first full bloom.

FURTHER READING

The book for this period always has been, always will be, Leslie Stephen's 1876 *History of English Thought in the Eighteenth Century*. Have we learned some things since? Yes. Has anybody used that new knowledge to craft a narrative with anything like the engaging prose and comprehensive familiarity that Stephen brought to the topic? Imma say no. Just listen to this description of the disparity between the prestige of the apologists and the clandestinity of the Deists:

"It would be difficult to mention a controversy in which there was a greater disparity of force. The physiognomy of the books themselves bears marks of the difference. The deist writings are but shabby and shriveled little octavos, generally anonymous, such as lurk in the corners of dusty shelves, and seem to be the predestined prey of moths. Against them are arrayed solid octavos and handsome quartos and at times even folios—very Goliaths among books, too ponderous for the indolence of our degenerate days, but fitting representatives of the learned dignitaries who compiled them."

I ask you—is that not gorgeous? Sentences that make for a good chaw. If you want more detail about Collins in particular, the only full length treatment I know of is *Anthony Collins: The Man and His Works* (1970) by James O'Higgins. It contains intense detail about the life of Collins and the battles of words he engaged in, and also incidentally has no style whatsoever. It is a series of pages with information encoded in word form. The information is good, and you won't get it anywhere else, but it's a fight.

Soul Man: La Mettrie's Great Step Forward

Soul Man: La Mettrie's Great Step Forward

For the nonbeliever, these are heady times: public debates, bestselling books, and a dizzying growth in both numbers and public presence all seem to suggest that history is swinging in an anti-clerical direction. It is astounding, but we've been in this position before. In the middle of the eighteenth-century religion was On The Run. A thin, perpetually ailing notary's son named Voltaire was, pamphlet by pamphlet, making bishops tremble, and his words found their way into the ears of the era's greatest monarchs and statesmen.

One hundred years later, it was all gone, replaced by a religious reordering of society and public life so pervasive that we are still battling with its ideals today. What happened? Is there a way to prevent it happening again? I can think of no better way to investigate the mystery than to start with the career of Julien Offray de la Mettrie (1709-1751), a French doctor and author whose arguments against the existence of the soul have been all but forgotten, wiped out in the great nineteenth-century religious revival and the adjustment of tactics by the philosophical community that followed.

La Mettrie, to those who know him at all, is remembered largely as a clownish figure at Frederick the Great's court whom neither Frederick nor Voltaire took seriously and who ended up dying early at the hands of bad paté. This is decidedly unjust. His early contributions to the so-called Doctor's Pamphlet War, in which he argued passionately for anatomical experience and accurate case studies over Galenic metaphysical speculation, were important in the advancement of French medicine in the eighteenth century. More than that, his 1748 work *Man, A Machine,* in the unflinching boldness with which it approached the most sacred of topics, man's possession of an immaterial soul, is possibly even more breathtaking today than it was in his own time.

La Mettrie's line of reasoning stemmed from his strict training in Hippocratean medical observation under the eighteenth century's most renowned physician, Herman Boerhaave. Against the reigning Cartesian soul-body dualism, which relied on thought experiments and logical extrapolations, La Mettrie compiled personal observations of his time as a physician to note the wide range of effects that purely physical ailments had on behavior and memory, two aspects of humans under the supposed purview of The Soul. Injury, disease, an alteration of diet, fatigue, intoxication—introduce any one of these severely enough, and the flavor of one's character starts inevitably to change. But if memory, behavior, and character are all so tied to the physical, what does that leave for a soul to actually do? La Mettrie concluded, "The soul is therefore but an empty word, of which no one has any idea, and which an enlightened man should only use to signify the part in us that thinks."

It took some time for La Mettrie's initial charge forward to be joined by the *philosophe* community, but within two decades after his death a united front had been formed. In 1764 Voltaire declared in his *Philosophical Dictionary* that the nature of the soul was not now, nor could it ever be, known. Baron d'Holbach followed suit in *The System of Nature* (1770), opining that, "Man is a being purely physical: the moral man is nothing more than this physical being considered under a certain point of view." That same year Denis Diderot wrote the essay *On Matter and Movement*, which furthered the materialist program by examining how matter could have force in and of itself, without being guided by outside spirits.

Interesting ideas all, but what the devil happened to them? The story of the snuffing of the French Revolution, and with it the return to that odd amalgam of Mysticism and Normalcy that would have its half-century under the sun as Victorianism and its offshoots, is common enough. The Revolution had touted its Enlightenment bona fides so vigorously that the fall of Robespierre could not but bring the fall of the philosophical school responsible for his rise. Skepticism of the La Mettrean mold was dropped because it was guilty by association, not because of a fundamental incompatibility with the coming Romanticism. You don't need to look farther than the late works of Beethoven to see what Might Have Been had the fusion of Enlightenment and Romanticism not been weighed down by the specter of the guillotine.

There is hope in this for us, because it means that as long as we can resist the urge to go about beheading monarchs and invading Austria, I think we'll be okay when it comes to engaging courageously and honestly with whatever neo-irrationalism the future has in store for us. After all, as machines go, we're terribly clever.

FURTHER READING
La Mettrie mainly shows up in the books of others, particularly in biographies of Frederick the Great and Voltaire, but if you want just La Mettrie you're pretty much limited to Kathleen Wellman's *La Mettrie: Medicine, Philosophy, and Enlightenment.*

For his original works, the Cambridge Texts in the History of Philosophy has an edition of *Man, a Machine* that includes a number of hard to find essays.

Hermann Samuel Reimarus:
The Man Who Exposed the Apostles

In 2013, Reza Aslan published a book, *Zealot*, with what was to have been the startling claim that Jesus thought of himself as primarily a temporal savior, whose image and mission were recast by his followers after he failed so profoundly at revolution. Was to have been, were it not for the tiny fact that this thesis was a by-the-numbers restatement of the work of eighteenth-century philologist and theologian Hermann Samuel Reimarus (1694-1768). That Aslan largely got away with the appropriation is a testament to how far Reimarus has sunk in the intellectual consciousness of the West. The initial publication of mere fragments of his work was a Europe-wide academic scandal of the first order and yet today, outside of the realm of Jesus historicity scholars, he is hardly ever quoted, his fascinating double-life as official theologian and hidden arch-skeptic rarely acknowledged.

In 1694, when Reimarus was born to a theologically inclined Hamburg family, Germany was teetering on the edge of intellectual revolution. Prior to 1650, German thought was wrapped primarily in the mystical and dogmatic ponderings of a group of dour Lutherans and Calvinists doing their level best to ignore the disturbing philosophical trends of England, France, and the Dutch Republic. But you can only keep Descartes out for so long, and thanks to two philosophical superstars, Gottfried Wilhelm Leibniz (1646-1716) and Christian Wolff (1679-1754), reason and critical investigation had a place again at the table. Their attempts to approach theology through reason, and to demonstrate the logical consistency of Christian belief, introduced new criteria of reasonableness into religious studies. While their conclusions were largely orthodox, their methods

represented a time bomb at the heart of German theology.

At first glance, nobody seems less likely than Hermann Reimarus to have been the man to touch off that explosion of critical theology. A student of religion and ancient languages, he was taught by one of Christianity's greatest apologists, Johann Albrecht Fabricius, who lived for compiling obscure early Christian texts and fighting vigorously all hints of biblical criticism. In 1728, Reimarus married Fabricius's niece, and, to all outward appearances, lived precisely the life of any ordinary German theological scholar, publishing books on logic and the truths of natural religion.

But inside, Reimarus was seething with a churning doubt. In 1720, he left Germany for a tour through the Netherlands and England, both centers of religious radicalism. Here, he had full access to the thoughts of Spinoza and English Deists like John Toland and Anthony Collins, who had elaborated criteria for the rejection of miracles in scripture and argued for the purely temporal nature of Jesus's mission. Returning to Germany, Reimarus ruminated on the evidence of internal contradiction in the Bible produced by the English, and investigated, using his knowledge of ancient languages, the validity of many of Christianity's favorite apologetic claims, finding them all wanting.

He had decided that Christianity's basic tenets were based on a set of self-serving fabrications constructed after Jesus's failed bid for earthly power, but dared not speak his mind. Germany was not England. J. Lorenz Schmidt had been arrested in 1735 for suggesting that revelation could be judged by reasonable investigation. A decade earlier, Wolff himself had been exiled by the Prussian king in spite of his internation-

al fame. Not only that, but his father-in-law was Johann Fabricius, the strong right arm of orthodox theology, and a man who could easily have ruined Reimarus's life if he felt that the young scholar had duped him to gain the hand of his daughter.

So, Reimarus praised Jesus in public and wrote the *Apologie oder Schutzschrift fuer die vernuenftigen Verehrer Gottes* in private. This mammoth work subjected the entirety of the Bible to a fierce rational critique, from the ubiquitous but sloppy miracles of the Old Testament to the massively contradictory accounts of Jesus's life and message in the New. Using his knowledge of linguistics, he traced the grammatical structures of different phrases to establish the original meaning of quotes that Christian apologists had deliberately muddied in order to make the Bible more internally consistent. His presentation of Jesus's use of the word "generation" alone is a *tour de force* of reasoning that settled, for anybody of reasonable mind, the apostles' belief in the imminent return of Jesus to earth.

By unearthing the linguistic conventions of the Jewish community in Jesus's time, Reimarus was able to explain the secular assumptions underlying Jesus's announcement of the coming "kingdom of heaven" and trace how those assumptions shed light on Jesus's later actions. This Jesus, Reimarus explains, was a man wholly in the model of previous Jewish zealots who had sought to overthrow the subjugation of the Jewish people, who had a good mind for popular psychology, but who spectacularly failed in his first real attempt to gain power. Jesus presented his purpose to the Jews in the familiar language of a new temporal kingdom, and his followers expected that they would sit next to him on the twelve thrones of earthly power he had promised.

Then he went and died having accomplished, by any objective criteria, nothing. So, a rewrite of the narrative was in order. The apostles, who had grown used to acclamation and the idea that they would rule nations, suddenly found themselves faced with the option of either modifying Jesus's message to make disaster appear as triumph, or of returning to the lowly jobs they had abandoned. Not surprisingly, they chose the former, and started crafting a notion of Jesus's resurrection, and of the universality of Jesus's message.

Jesus was no longer a temporal savior who had failed, but a cosmic, spiritual savior who was taking his time on coming back because of how grievous his suffering on the cross had been. Those quotes of his where he quite explicitly said that he came to preach to the Jews, and that the preservation of Jewish customs was paramount? Forget about all that. Everybody's invited now. As years passed and Jesus *still* didn't return, the apostles pushed back the clock on his imminence, even resorting to the "A hundred years for us is just an hour for him, so he's really not THAT late" argument that is somehow still in currency. In order to keep the religion going, after Jesus so fantastically made a hash of fulfilling the expectations of a Jewish Messiah, the apostles broadened the message to extend their potential base of power, and the results of that crass rebranding, from infant baptizing to transubstantiation to the Apocalypse, slowly became the basis for a new religion that had nothing whatsoever to do with what Jesus had initially attempted.

For a Germany that had just serenely convinced itself that religion either con-

formed to reason or was ethereally Above its dictates, the posthumous publication of excerpts from Reimarus's secret tome was a *Hadouken* wrapped in a thunderbolt. Between 1774 and 1778, Gotthold Ephraim Lessing (1729-1781) published seven selections under the title *Wolfenbuettel Fragments* (Wolfenbuettel had been where J. Lorenz Schmidt had died in exile, so the

title was likely an attempt to throw suspicion on Schmidt and away from Reimarus, whose family insisted on anonymity). They shocked the theological establishment so much for their radically impious approach to Jesus's mission and the hypocrisy of the apostles that the state demanded that Lessing hand over the manuscript, and never publish any of it, or indeed anything like it, again.

He didn't, and the full contents of the manuscript weren't made known again until David Friedrich Strauss wrote them up in his 1862 *Hermann Samuel Reimarus und Seine Schutzschrift fuer die Venuenftigen Verehrer Gottes* as part of his own attempt to critically reinvestigate the historicity of Jesus. Indeed, the publication of Reimarus's full text in any language has been something of a cursed undertaking, resulting in the relegation of Reimarus's name to the annals of Important Jesus Historians rather than the recognition of the daring contribution he made to religious studies generally. Faced with a nation of morbidly somber religiosity, he played his part dutifully while composing a work that looked the holy, untouchable apostles directly in the face and didn't flinch before calling them shameless fabricators of self-serving myths. He put Christian history on trial, demanding evidence that was consistent, asking questions of motivation that had been buried in false translations and shoddy narrative reworkings. His is a massively courageous book with a modest question at its core: Does the Bible make sense under a spiritual reckoning of Jesus? Reimarus refused the trite consolation of God's Mysterious Ways and answered, flatly, "No, probably not," and that made all the difference.

FURTHER READING

Reimarus continues to be plagued with problems in the availability of his works. The main readily available book in English is Charles H. Talbert's *Reimarus: Fragments*, which collects those parts of Reimarus that deal with Jesus's self-conception and with the manipulations undertaken by the apostles. Going further, you can pick up David Strauss's book on Reimarus in reprint editions. The ULAN press edition features mercifully large *Frakturschrift*, though the pixilation gets in the way at times, and there are somewhat mystically three copies of page 196. Still, the summary of the other parts of Reimarus's work is good to have.
For those curious about just how similar the central thesis of Aslan's *Zealot* and Reimarus's *Apologia* are, here is Aslan's summary of the purpose of his book:

"This book is an attempt to reclaim, as much as possible, the Jesus of history, the Jesus *before* Christianity: the politically conscious Jewish revolutionary who, two thousand years ago, walked across the Galilean countryside, gathering followers for a messianic movement with the goal of establishing the Kingdom of God but whose mission failed when, after a provocative entry into Jerusalem and a brazen attack on the Temple, he was arrested and executed by Rome for the crime of sedition. It is also about how, in the aftermath of Jesus's failure to establish God's reign on earth, his followers reinterpreted not only Jesus's mission and identity, but also the very nature and definition of the Jewish messiah."

And this is Reimarus, over two hundred years earlier:

"Thus the existing history of Jesus enlightens us more and more upon the object of his conduct and teaching, which entirely corresponds with the first idea entertained of him by his apostles, that is, that he was a *worldly* deliverer... It also shows that the master, and how much more his disciples, found themselves mistaken and deceived by the condemnation and death [of Jesus], and that the new system of a suffering spiritual savior, which no one had ever known or thought of before, was invented after the death of Jesus, and invented only because the first hopes had failed."

Hermann Samuel Reimarus is not mentioned once in the main body of *Zealot*, and in the Endnotes, only twice in passing, as being one Jesus historian among many, without reference to his central thesis.

Reason From Passion: David Hume, the Great Infidel

EDINBURGH, 1770.

DAVID HUME!

AYE?

OH, THAT'S RIGHT, YOU'RE SCOTTISH! QUICK, SAY "I DINNA THINK THE DILITHIUM CRYSTALS CAN TAKE MUCH MORE!"

YER' AN ODD BAIRN, I KEN. BUT I'VE NE'ER TURNED AWAY A MERRY LAD.

COOL, BECAUSE I HAVE QUESTIONS. LIKE, WHY ISN'T CAUSALITY REAL?

OH, IT'S THUMPING REAL, LAD. BUT DON'T YE FIND IT CURIOUS, JUST *HOW* WE CONNECT THE DOTS?

UMM, NO? WHY WOULD I?

ACH, YA BAWHEED! EFF YA LET PROXIMITY BECOME CAUSALITY SO EASY, THEN YE'LL LET THE POSSIBLE BE THE NECESSARY, AND HABIT BECOME TRUTH, WITHOUT THINKING HOW THINGS COULD BE DIFFERENT!

YE'LL LET PEOPLE SHAME YE, FER BEING A MAN, FER BEIN' 'APPY.

WOW, THAT'S PRETTY INSPIRING, DAVID HUME. IT JUST NEEDS ONE THING...

AYE? WHAT'S THAT?

YOU KNOW...

SIGH...I DINNA THINK THE DILITHIUM CRYSTALS CAN TAKE MUCH MORE.

YES! NOW, "OGRES HAVE LAYERS, ONIONS HAVE LAYERS"!

Humans are frightfully good at getting used to things. The phenomenal becomes the commonplace with depressing regularity, all newness sopped up and defused by our habit-prone brains. We devour novelty, reduce it to normalcy, and move mundanely on without a second thought. But what is the machinery of that process, of breaking down new experiences into old ones and cataloguing them, of routinizing the new? And what are the consequences of that mental machinery's operation?

The arc of those questions forms the intellectual life of one of humanism's greatest lights, the Scottish philosopher David Hume (1711-1776). While analyzing the formation of our mental habits, he uncovered new principles about the psychology of morality and the arbitrariness of religious certainty that earned him the epithet of The Great Infidel, and brought emotion and instinct crashing back into the realm of pure philosophy.

For the first forty years of his life, he was a man adrift, full of talent and startling ideas and with no idea whatsoever of how to apply them. He attended the University of Edinburgh at the age of twelve, showed himself a first-rank student, and then left before obtaining an actual degree. This was common practice at the time—you went to the university, brushed up on your Latin and classics, and then left when a chance at a real career offered itself, without troubling too much over the whole graduation thing.

Hume, however, didn't have a career waiting for him. He was a bookworm whose whole purpose was reading classics and refining the style of his written English, even as his spoken language was, and forever would be, a mass of (to an English ear) impenetrable Scotticisms. He was philosophically against the church, and didn't terribly fancy soldiering, which just left a career in trade, which he tried in 1734 for a few months, only to get summarily fired for systematically correcting the English of his employer's outgoing letters. So, he continued to drift, spending some time in France in the 1730s and even turning into an improbable military man when he accompanied General St. Clair on a farcical attempt to capture Lorient for no particular reason in 1746.

That's not to say that he was intellectually sterile during these years, just that the world seemed particularly dedicated to ignoring the revolutionary works of his mind and pen. His *A Treatise of Human Nature*, which he conceived while still a teenager but didn't manage to publish until 1739, was an archetypal misunderstood masterpiece. The force of its originality is still potent 270 years later, and it's no wonder that the few people who took notice of the book upon its first publication utterly failed to grasp its meaning.

The *Treatise* lays out the themes that Hume will elaborate for the rest of his career, and for pure youthful daring and novelty there are few books to equal it. Here he wonders about where reason and knowledge *really* fit into our behavior and societal assumptions, and his persistent question is, "Might things be otherwise?" All of our non-mathematical knowledge, he demonstrates, is based upon appeal to experience. We see one billiard ball strike a stationary ball, followed by the resultant motion of that stationary ball, and our brains stitch up the space in between those observations with causality. Prior to any experience with the transfer of momentum, we could imagine a thousand different effects resulting from the collision. Perhaps both balls stay still. Perhaps they both end up going backwards. Perhaps the second one leaps three feet up in the air. There is nothing in the motion of that first rolling ball which forces us, prior to experience, to expect a transfer of momentum and a resultant forward motion of the second ball. When we say *cause* we mean a temporal proximity of events that we have experienced enough times to link together mentally in a cause-effect system.

Hume's few early commentators took all this to mean that he believed that anything could cause anything, and that causality was a deep lie. They either deliberately or carelessly missed the subtlety of his parsing of how we intellectually experience causation. They couldn't see how he was, even as a teenager, sapping the walls of reality and common-sense reason, drawing attention to how we actively form our world by acts of unconscious mental creativity. And his critics certainly didn't appreciate his application of this skeptical system to morality.

Philosophy had been engaged, for a millennium or two, in the task of finding an absolute morality, a morality that had been perfected through reasonable argumentation until it rested at last in its ultimate form. Hume, melding his own insights into our unconscious smithing of reality with the emotional theories of Francis Hutcheson, maintained that this effort was not only impossible but undesirable, that morality comes not from some theoretical unified reason, but from a moral sense lodged in the motive powers of sympathy and self-interest. Passion, that maligned and "brutish" feature of humanity, Hume locates at the center of our moral creativity, and suggests that, so long as moral theory disdainfully does without the input of sympathetic instinct in favor of theological or philosophical perfection, it will only be a hobbling approximation entirely incapable of explaining the growth and evolution of societal morality.

This new morality was distinctly *not* appreciated.

Shaken by the critical and financial failure of the *Treatise,* Hume experimented with the form of the essay, gaining success by publishing a series of moral and political short pieces attuned to the essay-mania of the mid eighteenth century. Buoyed by the reception of those works, he reworked the *Treatise* in several less-abstract forms, including the *Essay Concerning Human Understanding*, which contained the new sections, *Of Miracles* and *Of a Particular Providence and of a Future State,* both of which alerted the clergy who weren't already in the know to the implications of Humean thought for theology.

British theologians had been having a hard enough time fighting off the English Deists, but had been holding their own (or so they felt) so long as the ground of conflict was the historical position of the church and interpretation of the scripture. With Hume, however, a new front had been opened, a concentrated and philosophically formidable attack on every possibility of religious certainty. Hume had, through the growing popularity of his essays, gone from an abstract non-entity to a religious threat greater than Voltaire, Diderot, and all the English Deists put together.

The best place to see what they were so scared of is in Hume's *Dialogues Concerning Natural Religion*, which he considered the finest of all his writings, but which his friends wouldn't let him publish during his life. Written largely in the 1750s, it is a conversation between an orthodox theist, a philosophical theist, and a skeptic, and it is devastating. The majority of the book is given over to a sustained analysis of the Argument From Design, the argument that, since a watch needs a watchmaker, therefore the universe, being ever more intricate than a watch, must have a supreme designer, which is God.

Hume quickly summarizes the easy objection to this argument, that it rests on analogy, and that arguments by analogy are only as good as the two items being compared are similar, and that the act of creating a watch and that of creating a universe are so wholly different that all sense of proportion rails against analogous treatment. He then moves into a virtuoso display of ingenuity that could have come from no one but David Hume. He steps back from the blatant anthropomorphism of the Argument from Design to point out that selecting design as an analogical starting point is essentially arbitrary: "What peculiar privilege has this little agitation of the brain which we call *thought,* that we must thus make it the model of the whole universe?" He then proceeds to spin with dizzying novelty a series of alternate cosmogonies, based on analogy from other observable aspects of nature.

If you analogize backwards not from design, but from vegetative generation, you get a model of a succession of universes producing each other mechanically, as a tree produces seeds which produce new trees. If you choose to focus on how finite goals are produced from the contributions of multiple finite entities, you create a polytheistic cosmogony. Looked at evolutionarily, perhaps the Earth is the first experiment of a limited God who hasn't quite figured the whole process out. Taking gravity and magnetism as your central analogical objects, perhaps motion and attraction can generate order from within, and that therefore the universe is its own God. With unchecked mirth, he rolls through the possibilities, and demonstrates how each is, under the conventions of analogical reasoning upon which the Argument from Design rests, equally likely. To construct a whole cosmogony on man's design of machines is about as fruitful as constructing one on a plant's ability to produce seeds, or a constructions crew's ability to specialize tasks to create a unified and diverse object— they are all equally probable, analogically speaking, and therefore none of them are certain or necessarily compelling.

It was that same capacity of stepping back from habit to conceive of how a system appears before we have habituated ourselves to its premises that sparked the controversial ingenuity of the *Treatise* and that devastated religious orthodoxy in the *Dialogues* and a small clutch of other works besides. Hume's sharp capacity to stab at unperceived weak spots in the very concept of Certainty itself made him a dangerous enemy of intellectual conformity, who used his increasing reputation to speak out in favor of man's right to suicide, against all forms of organized religion, and for the world-changing power of applied empathy.

But what was really the final insult of all was that David Hume, the arch-heretic, was at the same time considered the most delightful man one could possibly befriend. Many of his closest friends were priests and theologians who abhorred the powerful skepticism of his writings, but who could not help but loving the man personally. The Great Infidel was at the same time *le bon*

David, whose reputation for basic goodness and mildness of temper was beyond question. Upon his return to France as a diplomatic secretary in the 1760s, he was greeted as a national hero by king, commoner, priest, and atheist alike. When he was attacked in the press, it was the moderate clergy of Scotland who were the first to rise to his defense. Even James Boswell, who as friend to Dr. Johnson ought to have reviled Hume, couldn't help but attend the Great Infidel in his final sickness, to sit and wonder at how a man with no sense of religion could remain so composed and even cheerful in the face of death.

Hume put to an end the idea that irreligion and personal immorality must necessarily go hand in hand. For a Britain that had taught itself that there was something low and vicious about the English Deists, David Hume was the first great public example of a man entirely and publicly without religion who was nonetheless happy, moral, and internationally venerated. His *History of England* was the standard text for a century after his death. George III honored him with a pension and a position as diplomatic *chargé d'affaires* in France and then as Under Secretary in England, setting a precedent for allowing the avowedly irreligious to serve with distinction in government. As a philosopher, we owe Hume much, but as a human, we owe him the birth of our public efficacy.

FURTHER READING

The Life of David Hume by E.C. Mossner (1954) has been the Hume book of record for a while now, and for good reason. In spite of stretching to a considerable six hundred pages of often dense font, its total grasp of Hume's life and political/intellectual world are not only beyond question, but delivered with a humor and appreciation of humanity that you don't often find. To paraphrase Captain Kirk, of all the books I've encountered in my studies, his was the most... Hume-an. (sorry) There is also an intriguing new work by James A. Harris, *Hume: An Intellectual Biography* (2015), which is also the requisite six hundred pages but which, at $55 a copy, is too rich for my blood. I'll let you know about it when the paperback comes out.

If religion is a single, concentrated expression of authority, humanism is the modest accumulation of a million small acts. It is the stuff of daily living—of being understanding when you could be righteous, of allowing people to live and love as they are, of seeing cosmic futility everywhere but pressing on anyway. Small things, personal moments which, aggregated, make civilization function at its steady and forgiving best.

Charming, but hardly the stuff of epics, surely. At least that was the verdict of a few odd centuries, when humanism spoke through essays and brief tales and hushed epigrams, bursts of reason that dared hope for nothing higher than a couplet, fearfully tendered. But all that while, civilization was cooking a man, somebody who combined verse, vision, cunning, and chutzpah in such forceful unity that, at last, an epic of toleration might be sung. After 1694 years of waiting, the world baked us a Voltaire.

For humanists, Voltaire (1694-1778) is the touchstone, the indispensable element of our common ancestry. What Mozart is to classical music, and *The Legend of Zelda* to video game nerdery, Voltaire is to humanism, our fond example of what we are when we are at our best. Surveying the first half of his life, however, that warm posterity appears anything but assured. His plays failed more often than they succeeded. He was jailed twice, and exiled for years at a time. He was given credit for mediocre works he did not write, and prevented from claiming credit for those he did. He was physically beaten on two occasions and received scant to no justice on account of his low social status. Except for a short stretch in a ramshackle apartment, he had no lodgings of his own, but bounced aimlessly from chateau to chateau, buffeted by blind chance, the malice of the Parisian public, and the whims of the ruling elite.

The inconstancy and spite of Paris could be overwhelming. It pushed J.J. Rousseau into simmering madness and paranoia, and ground mediocrities into scornful oblivion. But Voltaire was unsinkable, and his upbringing points to why. His father was a dutiful and practical notary, his mother a sparkling and educated conversationalist. For us, "notary" exists with "real estate agent" and "fingerprint technician" as a sort of civilizational flotsam constantly on the verge of being replaced by indifferent machines or cleverer-than-average apes. In seventeenth-century France, however, notaries were powerful community keystones. They were there at every significant life event to render it official. They had connections with every stratum of society. They loaned money to princes, and carried the secrets of kings. Voltaire's father was very successful in his honorable profession, and expected his children to augment the family name, either as notaries themselves, or perhaps as solicitors.

Seldom have a father's expectations been so thoroughly trammeled. Of his two sons, one was a Jansenist bigot who believed in convulsionism and miracles and hair shirts, and the other, François-Marie Arouet, our Voltaire, a society wag who depended on the popularity of his *bon mots* for food and lodging. Voltaire's mother died when he was only seven years old, but in that short time she attracted a circle of admirers who placed their stamp upon the young prodigy. The schoolbooks teach us that the latter half of Louis XIV's reign was a dreary expanse of expensive wars and religious hyper-orthodoxy, and so it was officially, but beneath the surface was a crackling ocean of freethought, dominated by decidedly earthly abbés who supported monasteries financially in exchange for a title, and who privately wrote scathing attacks on Christianity amidst quite literal orgies. Voltaire's mother knew a few of these men, and they brought the young child not only the beloved pagan classics of antiquity, but recent works like *La Moïsade*, a religious satire of enormous but secret popularity.

To put his son on track to be a proper solicitor, *père* Voltaire sent him to the *Collège Louis le Grand*, a Jesuit school of the highest standing which offered a thorough education in the fripperies of religion, in staging dramatic productions, in Latin and a smidge of Greek, and in nothing useful whatsoever. During his time there, Voltaire shone for his facility with impromptu verse and his daring intelligence made palatable by his superfluity of easy charm. The scholars, while Jesuits, were lovers of antiquities cut from much the same cloth as his mother's abbé friends, and tolerated Voltaire's occasional impieties for the sake of his sparkling poems and honest love of the works of the Roman past. And so, though he was sent to school to learn to become a sober solicitor, what he learned in fact was how to be a charming courtier and dazzling poet. Modern history, mathematics, science, current languages, finance—of these he knew next to nothing, and would spend the rest of his life vigorously making up for these six lost years of education.

Having been lauded and petted for his wit and verse, the young Voltaire was thoroughly unwilling to settle down to the routine of an apprentice solicitor. His father secured him a number of promising positions which the youth frittered away, choosing to spend his time fashioning poems and attending gatherings of high society vivants rather than sedulously copying legal documents. He was given the chance to accompany the Dutch ambassador on an official visit to Holland, only to end it in house arrest and a precipitous drubbing out of that country on account of his attempts to elope with a local beauty named, and this is true, Pimpette. Irresponsible, broke, lovestruck, his eighteen-year-old breast full of passionate sentiments expressed in the high style, Voltaire returned to Paris in disgrace.

In disgrace, but not beaten. Almost immediately upon arriving in Paris, he started enlisting the help of his Jesuit contacts, spinning them a tragic tale of Pimpette being kept under house arrest by her Protestant relations, urging them to use their authority to extricate her from Holland and bring her to France, painting himself as merely a disinterested and dutiful son of Catholicism while conveniently neglecting to mention his *real* purpose. He was soon found out, the lady moved on to greener pastures, and his father disinherited him. Yet, so long as he was clever, he always had a spot at a well-stocked table, a sumptuous meal just a flattering epigram away.

The problem with being the wittiest of the wits, of course, is that anytime anything biting and anonymous is said, it's attributed to you, the same way that, back in the days of Napster, *every* parody song listed Weird Al Yankovic as the artist. And so it came to pass that, when a new set of verses describing an incestuous relationship between the regent of France and his daughter surfaced, they were officially ascribed to Voltaire, and the poet was clapped in the Bastille for eleven months without possibility of defense or release except at the regent's pleasure.

But before we weep too many tears, you have to realize that the Bastille was not a hole of misery where prisoners fed off rats and darkness. Voltaire had a fireplace with plenty of wood, three positively sumptuous meals a day, access to visitors, the freedom to eat at the governor's table, whatever books and comforts from home he might like, in short everything he could want save pen and paper, lest he write more wicked poems in his leisure hours (he wrote anyway, just in his head, composing huge sections of the epic *L'Henriade* then memorizing them). In many ways, until he finally came to rest with Madame du Châtelet at Cirey, this time in the Bastille was the most stable and restful that he would know. When another author stepped forward and admitted to having penned the noxious lines, Voltaire was released, and what was more, his time in the Bastille had made him more popular than ever, so popular that he could finally have his first play put on the stage: *Oedipe*, a refashioning of the Sophocles tragedy in the grand French style.

It was a monstrous hit which made Voltaire's name as something more than just a dining room prattler. He was an author now, and would continue writing under the most trying of conditions for the rest of his life. As sure of a success as *Oedipe* was, however, his next two plays were thundering flops, and it is entirely possible that Voltaire would have drifted back into fashionable obscurity had his mouth not gotten him into trouble, again. It happened that a useless noble of respected family, the chevalier de Rohan, took it into his head to limply tease Voltaire about having changed his name from Arouet to Voltaire. Rohan approached the author at the theater one evening and made some comment about not knowing how to address him. Voltaire, we imagine, raised an eyebrow and let the matter slide, until another performance when Rohan went into Voltaire's box and made, more or less, the same comment, to which Voltaire responded, according to what version you believe, with either, "I do not trail a great name after me, but at least I know how to honor the name I bear" or "I begin my name, whereas you are the end of yours." The chevalier left in a huff, gathered together some hired thugs, and had them call on Voltaire. They lured the unsuspecting

poet out into the street, and then viciously beat him in the open air, while the chevalier barked out instructions for the pummeling from the safety of a nearby carriage.

Voltaire demanded justice from the law, but everywhere he turned he was confronted with the fact that the chevalier was a chevalier, and he was a playwright, and that therefore no action would be taken. He would have to walk the streets of Paris, listening to the laughter from every corner as children identified him as the poet who was so unimportant that he could be beaten with impunity. Voltaire rankled under the indignity, and hired a fencing master to teach him the art of the blade so that he could demand satisfaction from the cowardly chevalier. All the while, however, his movements were being carefully watched, and as soon as he made an official challenge, the police were at his door and he was once more in the Bastille which was, probably, the best thing for him. Had the duel proceeded, Rohan would have sliced him to pieces, and the public would have gone on with its business. But as a prisoner, public opinion swung back round to his favor, and Rohan was reviled.

Sensing the unofficial sympathy to his plight, Voltaire asked to be allowed to exile himself to England, a request readily granted. And so, a chain which began with a witless noble trying to prove himself a wag ended with Voltaire traveling to the one place in the world that could teach him what he needed to evolve from a promising dramatist to a world-class historian and social commentator.

England was everything that France was not. Where in France a man could spend eleven months in prison for something he didn't even write, England's relative liberty of the press was a revelation. France's ob-session with titles and rank, which Voltaire had just experienced firsthand, gave way in England to an aristocracy of mind. When Newton died a year after Voltaire's arrival, his coffin was carried by noble hands to a grave beside kings, an event inconceivable in Bourbon France. And not only was England the land of political liberality and intellectual aristocracy, it was the land of Shakespeare.

Nobody and nothing confused, repelled, and attracted Voltaire like Shakespeare. Coming from the French drama, with its iron rules, Shakespeare seemed barbarous. A French play had to, by established custom, take place in one location, the action taking place in real time, and the characters being noblemen and deities. Shakespeare was incomprehensible from such a standpoint. Ghosts and gravediggers and murder and psychological ruminations—dramatic blasphemy! And yet... to a playwright whose last two works failed, this barbarism was seductive, and the plays he wrote after returning to France slowly, but with a gathering momentum, broke rules and introduced supernatural and exotic elements that the young Voltaire would have contemptuously scorned.

But England's lasting impact was on Voltaire's opinion of what life and society are about. The towering power of tolerance to construct a society of mutual respect and admiration for actual, rather than inherited, merit was massively instructive, and would form the matter of Voltaire's social works for the rest of his life. He had been writing, since his first Bastille imprisonment, an epic poem on the reign of Henri IV, which lauded the king's famous tolerance in the face of the religious brutalities of the St. Bartholomew's Day Massacre and the wars of the Catholic League. *L'Henriade* is the *Aeneid* of humanism, the parallels between the two being quite consciously intended by Voltaire. It is, in terms of grand sentiment harnessed in the cause of modesty and cultural unity, unsurpassed to this day, the sureness of Voltaire's poetic sense married perfectly to the scale of his vision. But after England, Voltaire found yet a new means of expressing his thoughts about the humanity-sundering nature of Christianity as against the frothy happiness of baseline humanity—prose.

First in the *English Letters*, and then later in the *Philosophical Dictionary* and ultimately in his masterwork of late life, *Candide*, Voltaire dared to make skepticism light and enjoyable. His histories, of Charles XII and Louis XIV, blazed the way for an approach to history that focused on intellectual trends and societal change first, and the foibles of rulers and results of battles a distant second. His cultural essays showed the French what could be, if they let their racial disdain for all things English lapse long enough to learn something from a society dedicated to freedom of conscience. His satires of religious zealotry, from his second epic poem, *La Pucelle*, a bawdy and scurrilous rewriting of the history of Joan of Arc, to his culturally relativist plays, like *Zaire* and *Alzire*, showed a most Christian continent what its superstitions looked like outside of their native soil.

Returning to France, he was the author everybody *must* read, if secretly. The court loved the *Henriade*, even if officially they couldn't approve it at first. Every respectable society female simply *had* to have a hidden copy of the semi-pornographic *La Pucelle*, and Voltaire's broadsides aimed at the pretensions of his fellow French intellectuals, such as *The Temple of Taste*, were greeted with wild enthusiasm. All was going so well, it was high time for it to all fall apart again, in typical Voltaire fashion. Copies of his *English Letters* leaked into France, containing the full measure of the author's scorn for Catholic absurdity, Pascalean pleasure hatred, and royal pretension. His lauding of intellectual liberty and religious toleration struck the court as treasonous, and Voltaire was forced to flee France anew.

To the house of his lover, the brilliant Madame du Châtelet, at Cirey in Champagne, then just outside of the French borders. There he lived in absolute contentment with his lover, her obliging husband, and their children, a perfect family unit not uncommon for the time. Châtelet was one of the continent's greatest mathematicians, a polylingual genius whose commentaries on Newton broke down French resistance to the Englishman's gravitational theories. They spent their days together performing science experiments on the nature of heat, reading English essays, and writing masterworks. He was having so much fun, in fact, that even though he could return to Paris thanks to a wholly insincere disavowal of authorship of the *English Letters*. "They say I must retract. Very willingly. I will declare that Pascal is always right; that if St. Luke and St. Mark contradict one another it is a proof of the truth of religion to those who know well how to take things; that another lovely proof of religion is that it is unintelligible; that Jesuits are honest people; that monks are neither proud, nor given to intrigue, nor stinking; that the holy inquisition is the triumph of humanity and tolerance. In a word, I will say all that is desired of me, provided that they will leave me in repose." He chose to remain in Cirey, and was happy there until that insincerity caught up with him.

The printer who had been jailed for publishing the *English Letters* wanted Voltaire to compensate him for his losses. Voltaire acknowledged authorship in a private response letter, and said he would pay half of the printer's asking price. The printer saw his opportunity and, incriminating letter in hand, brought suit against Voltaire. It was a disgraceful business that Voltaire ended up legally winning, but at the expense of all public esteem. He was largely seen as a rich bully who made others lie to protect his own reputation, and when he returned to Cirey it was as a man thoroughly rejected by his audience and government, a scoundrel who would never be trusted again. In the depths of that defeat, he came home, and found waiting for him a letter from an enthusiastic young prince, a letter full of fulsome, almost servile, praise for his work. The prince's name was Frederick.

FURTHER READING

There is a wealth of material available about Voltaire. My favorite biography is Parton's two-volume work from 1886. The prose is engaging, and the depth of detail immaculate. More recently, *Voltaire: Genius of Mockery* by Victor Thaddeus (1928) is a nice one-volume work, with Robert Wagoner's slim translation of Gustave Lanson's classic work being a good general purpose introduction. People talk up Theodore Besterman's 1969 *Voltaire,* but it comes down pretty hard on *L'Henriade,* which I've never quite forgiven it for, even if its points are largely just.

EPISODE
29

One Poet Against Christendom. Voltaire,
Part II: The People's Hero

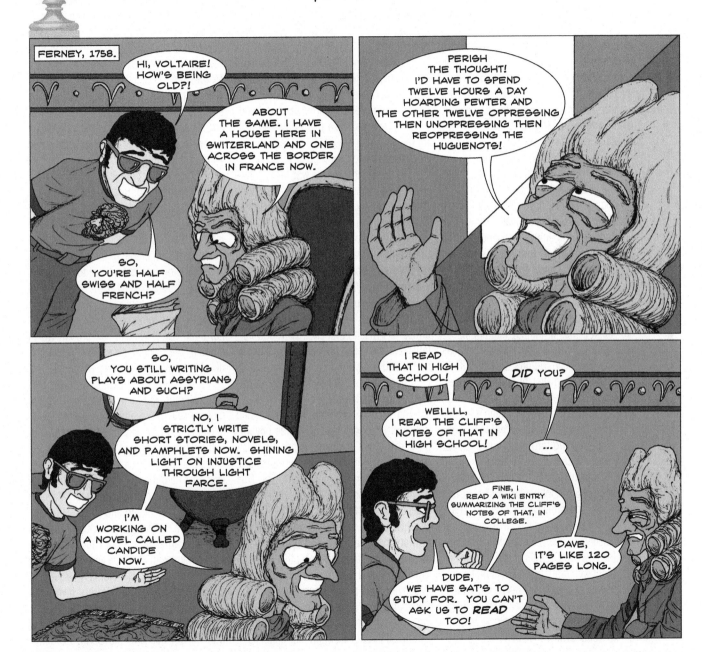

For three decades, Voltaire and Frederick the Great formed the intellectual-political axis about which Europe spun. Voltaire's *bon mots* and pamphlets created the moral conscience of a generation even as Frederick's wars and cynical worldview forged its political boundaries. Their correspondence is an elegant labyrinth shifting between mutual, overtly homoerotic hero worship and bemused disdain. By Voltaire's death in 1778, he was the indispensable intellectual leader of the continent and the hero of the people, and Frederick mourned him ironically from atop his lonely throne.

But what remains of Voltaire now?

Today, he is the guy who wrote *Candide*, that book you read in your undergraduate Humanities sequence during Enlightenment Week. Everything else—the plays that captivated a continent for a century and a half, the histories that changed how historical research was done, the short stories and pamphlets that put the desperate social issues of the day into approachable, comic terms– *everything* else, has vanished from civilization's ready recall.

Partly, it's a matter of changing tastes. As revolutionary as Voltaire's plays were in their injection of Shakespearean strangeness into the ossified classical French drama, their rhyming formalism has been out of favor for a century now, and the elegant art of correspondence, of which Voltaire was the undisputed continental master, is one we couldn't possibly care less about. That's changing under the maxim that everything dead becomes charming again eventually, and the flowering of interest in Baroque opera might well drag the classicism of eighteenth-century drama and *belles lettres* with it, but I doubt the wildest optimist anticipates the return of *The Scotch Woman* to the floorboards anytime soon.

Partly, though, the decline is a result of Voltaire's conscious decision to act through a million bothersome pinpricks rather than via grand declamations. If the first half of his life was about epic verse, clever table prattle, and gossip-inducing dramas, the second was about locking horns with the titanic social injustices of the day through pamphlets, novels, and letters, educating the common people in terms they could understand and organize themselves around, for the reform of the justice system and the ridicule of religious pomposity.

The road to this rebirth was brutal, however, and perhaps needed to be. Misfortune and disillusion broke down Voltaire's taste for the stunning world of high society acclaim, and sharpened his wit, allowing him to become a devastatingly effective scourge of privilege. Embarrassed by the legal fiasco over the *English Letters*, Voltaire decided to build up his political capital by solidifying his relationship with the fawning crown prince of Prussia, Frederick. Through flattery no less abject for being mostly sincere, he praised the young prince's idealism to the firmament, and made sure their correspondence was known.

The French authorities took note and Voltaire's situation bettered as the government realized it might influence Prussian policy through its errant playwright's hold upon the mercurial, pro-French royal. This connection helped smooth the way for the acceptance of *Mahomet*, a 1741 play that clearly used the cynical religious chicanery of Mohammed as a screen for commenting on the violent and deceptive heart of Christianity, and which he artfully managed to convince the pope to endorse as a Very Christian Work. It's a powerful and disturbing work still, and it will probably not be performed in English within our lifetimes.

For years, he had a stable home and regular routine at the home of Madame du Châtelet and then that astounding woman, who brought Newton's full significance to France, died in 1749 after giving birth to the child of her tertiary lover, an officer poet who quite harmoniously shared her with the Marquis and Voltaire (France, right?). After years of productive and occasionally stifling stability, Voltaire had to find a new home, and Frederick the Great was there, throwing money and prestige at him if only he would come and live in Prussia.

Frederick's court was precisely what Voltaire needed to undertake his late-life metamorphosis into the people's hero. Where at Paris, one was liable to be thrown into the Bastille for impertinence at a moment's notice, at Frederick's table a complete and sparkling intellectual freedom reigned. Avowed atheists like La Mettrie spoke the full measure of their conviction, with Frederick merrily encouraging each dizzy impropriety. For three years, Voltaire saw a court where nothing was sacred except the monarch's duty to improve the lot of his people.

It was here that Voltaire wrote his history of Louis XIV, a work that defined the modern role of research and source skepticism in historical authorship, and which put cultural trends ahead of military ones as the focus of civilization. It was also here, however, that he did a number of foolish things à la Voltaire which were decidedly beneath a person of his wealth and status. He speculated in a scheme to essentially defraud the Prussian state. He got caught up in an ugly lawsuit with a Jew he was more or less trying to swindle. He clumsily attempted to play the role of spy to curry favor with the French government. He picked an unflattering if hilarious fight out of jealousy with the president of the Berlin Academy,

Maupertuis, a man he recommended for the position in the first place.

Who can say what drove Voltaire to these compulsive effronteries? He was economically cunning, and couldn't pass up a good deal, which made him the wealthiest literary figure of his, or perhaps any, time, but also got him entangled in shady and lowly schemes. Frederick was tolerant at first, but as Voltaire's public attacks on his Academy president grew more ferocious, a line needed to be drawn. Voltaire left in a huff, but took a collection of Frederick's verse with him, verse which contained enough inflammatory material to set the courts of Europe solidly against Prussia. Frederick had him stopped and arrested until he gave up the volume, and an over-zealous official kept Voltaire in bureaucratic and penal limbo for weeks before word got to Frederick, and Voltaire was freed.

It was the Rohan Beating Incident all over again, a stinging reminder of just how little power Voltaire actually had when it came to his own safety and security. Humbled and homeless, having lived three years in an intellectual climate that backed down before no idol, Voltaire was ready at last to sensibly refashion his life. He fled to Switzerland and bought an estate of his own and then bought another just across the French border. These dual households were to be his protection the rest of his life—the French house was where he entertained and put on the plays that were forbidden by the joyless Calvinist authorities of Switzerland, while the Swiss house was the refuge he could retreat to at a moment's notice when the French authorities threatened him with arrest. He was, at long last, untouchable, and it freed him to speak the full measure of his mind at last.

This was the Voltaire of the battle-cry Écrasez l'infâme! The Voltaire who backed the judicial system of France into a corner time and time again, forcing them to repeal their medieval rulings and reinvestigate the role that purely religious offenses ought to play in the legal system. He used every connection he had, and poured out a steady flood of money, to defend religious minorities persecuted in France. In the Calas case, a Protestant was accused of murdering his son for wanting to convert to Catholicism. The evidence clearly showed that the death was a suicide, but the religious bigotry of the courts demanded Calas's life, and he was broken on the wheel, tortured to death, for the crime of Being Protestant In France. Voltaire, hearing of the case, sprung to action, compelled the French courts to reopen the case, and eventually to clear the father's name so that his family could have whatever semblance of a normal life was left to them. Throughout France, Voltaire was known as the Hero of Calas, and each subsequent case he championed deepened the people's love of their distant defender.

He wrote brief pamphlets and short novels needling religion and government for their various pomposities and manifest cruelties, a flotilla of small works that flooded the coping mechanisms of French censorship, and found their way into every corner of an increasingly revolutionary France. Like the English Deists, he reveled in drawing comparisons between Christian and Chinese civilization, using the elegance and antiquity of the latter to throw dust at the pretensions of the former. He called attention to the arbitrariness of French law and argued persuasively for reforms in divorce law, a reversal of the wealthy's privileged legal position, the abolition of torture during the carrying out of a death penalty, and the complete removal of religious offenses from the legal system.

And along the way, he produced *Candide* (1759), a masterpiece of constructive mockery that tore to tatters any philosophical system which would appeal to God's magnificent design to justify the obvious cruelties of existence. It was uproarious then, and hilarious still. It unrolls the barbarity of European civilization, sparing no nation or tradition in its cataloging of our brilliantly loathsome misuse of each other. It's formally a sustained attack on the philosophy of Leibniz, but in reality it is a deliciously wicked romp illustrating the indifference of the universe to our plight, ending in what is perhaps *the* motto of modern humanism: forget the claims to omnipotence of religion, the vagaries of royal puffery, and all notions of glorious combat, and turn to the community around you, to improving life for those you can directly help. Cultivate your garden.

Voltaire's life of exile and disillusionment had, after all, a storybook ending. Aged 84, he returned in 1778 to Paris, and a triumph. Beloved by the people, toasted by the intellectual community, the city fell over itself to do him honor. He died within months of his return, having been given an ovation at the Academie, and watched his most recent play rapturously received. His was the wit that stung Europe's most powerful nation into a shambling reformation that would soon accelerate into full revolution, and that dared treat religion's contradictions and obfuscations in a global context that highlighted Christianity's simultaneous triviality and barbarism. If the humanism of today is a gallant mixture of knowing effrontery, global consciousness, and over-the-top mockery, it's because Voltaire made it so, and we have yet to find the role model to displace him.

Making Determinism Art: The Humanist Fictionscapes of Denis Diderot

By the mid-eighteenth century, materialism and its close cousin determinism both had august philosophical traditions behind them. Hobbes, Spinoza, Collins, and La Mettrie had all made convincing arguments about the nonexistence of the soul, and effected breaches in mankind's natural reluctance to part with the notion of free will. But a convincing argument for why you *ought* to believe something is often no help at all in figuring out how one is to *live* with that belief. How do you accept yourself as a mechanical automaton and still laugh and love and create and strive? It would take somebody with the sharp mind of a philosopher and the boundless imagination of a literary dreamer to finally give us, in an artistic medium that people could readily grasp and understand, our first answers to that question.

Pre-Revolutionary France had no shortage of contestants in the race to be that somebody. Voltaire and Rousseau (and to a less literary degree d'Alembert, d'Holbach, Condillac, and Helvetius) all had profound things to say about man's new relation to himself in the light of the Age of Reason. Yet their works, stunning as they often were, show a beholdenness to the conventions of their time which prevented the potential of the new philosophy from being fully realized. To avoid crippling philosophy by chaining it to the prejudices of *ancien régime* narrative strictures, a more subversive literary thinker was needed, a man willing to break the bones of the traditional novel and reset them according to his own creative whim and insight.

The man fated to accomplish this task was Denis Diderot (1713-1784), who famously gave decades of his life to editing the grand *Encylopédie* which represented the zenith of the *philosophe* tradition's hopes for the classification and dissemination of the world's knowledge. He was an avowed atheist, determinist, and materialist, a ceaseless talker known for vigorously gesticulating to the point of injuring his conversational neighbors, a man willing to undertake any task for a friend, and a man who was able to delight in the surprising creations of his mental powers precisely because he recognized how deeply foreign he was to himself.

Were you to consider Diderot based on his published work at the time of his death, you would think him a diligent editor, a passable playwright, and a vigorous and clever essayist, and then promptly move on to talking about the wicked cleverness of Voltaire or the tragic sentimentality of Rousseau. For Diderot, somewhat oddly for a man so obsessed with the notion of reputation, kept his works of true genius under tight wrap, and many were not widely known until decades after his death. *Jacques the Fatalist, D'Alembert's Dream*, and *Rameau's Nephew*, the three masterpieces that form the base of his literary reputation today, were familiar to only a handful during Diderot's life, and even when editions began emerging in the nineteenth century, they failed to ignite the imagination of an age that was interested in nothing so much as lying in the cozy lap of sentiment, where messy ruminations about identity dared not indecently tread.

It took us the better part of two centuries to rediscover Diderot, to open *Jacques* and realize at once that here was the person who had not only grappled with the anxieties of modernist philosophy, but who was able to do it artistically, through a recasting of formal elements, in a way that the giants of the early twentieth century were only stumblingly working out afresh for themselves.

Diderot's question is, in all three of these novels, "How do you live, knowing what you know?" In *D'Alembert's Dream*, the action of the novel's middle section revolves around the words spoken by a sleeping d'Alembert, as relayed to his doctor by his lover. It is, already, a strangely modern configuration, where the main character is only allowed to represent himself through a disconnected dream fugue, while lover and doctor push his thoughts this way and that in his eerily absent presence. D'Alembert's ravings center on identity and materialism—how are we to think of ourselves? As a unity, a duality, a swarm of cooperating interests? Where are "we" in the whole mess of tissues and organs, or is that even an important question? More practically, what changes when we accept at last that we are matter pushed forward on a wave of continuous reactions? This last question is answered with true Diderot charm when the lover and the doctor finally sit down to explore, with unhindered curiosity, the consequences of D'Alembert's night musings—discovering for themselves how much there is to gain in demystifying the body's nature, how much more capacity for pleasure, and less for fruitless shame.

What *D'Alembert* did in humanizing materialism, *Jacques the Fatalist* and *Rameau's Nephew* did for determinism. In *Rameau,* the incorrigible nephew of the great composer Jean-Philippe Rameau is depicted in conversation with, effectively, Diderot himself, though it's probably more accurate to say that the two characters rep-

single person's role within it. He is a gifted pantomime artist with utterly no certainty about his identity, given to paradox after paradox, any of which would be perfectly at home in a Jean Genet play. But Diderot can't bring himself to let that side of the rationalist mentality win the day—he fights against the implications to find a happiness in a posterity that he knows he will never behold, in a humanity mechanically hurtling into the void, but doing so with a set of instincts that are beautiful and worth lauding even as the cynics snicker. Little wonder that the book didn't find its posthumous audience until the self-sure era of Romanticism passed and the age of troubling questioning scrambled forward, looking for a guide, any guide, about what to do with itself and its terrible self-knowledge.

It's a great book, but of another order entirely is *Jacques the Fatalist and His Master*. It is, truth be told, my favorite book. It breaks all the rules as narrator, reader, Jacques, and his Master all vie for control of the storytelling process, getting in each other's way, making their demands, staking their rights to existence and independence, all creating a mad whirl of stories begun and interrupted, narrative expectations thwarted, and a great number of things insistently Not Happening when, by any standard of literary decency, they ought. It is so inventive and gleefully subversive, that any other work of the eighteenth century read afterwards must appear somewhat flat and ordinary by comparison. Even *Candide,* brilliant as it is, can't long stand next to the joyful madness of *Jacques*.

It's a perfect case of form and message seamlessly wound into each other. For Jacques is something of a confirmed Spinozist, a servant living his life in the full

resent two halves of Diderot's character, set in opposition so that Diderot can, through art, sort his contradictory modern psyche out. On the one side is the part of him that loves knavery and abhors pretense, the perpetually bankrupt cynic who dances to the tune of his temporary masters and repays them in veiled impertinence, and who knows that his greatest insincerity comes when he insists on being sincere. This side is represented by the nephew character, while the "Diderot" character represents all of his benevolent impulses, his optimism for the future and belief in virtue and justice, his need

to see humanity amount to something and to be part of that process.

In their back and forth, they reenact dramatically the conversation that I think every humanist engages in privately—what to do with one's self in a doomed world. Rameau's nephew sees all the pettiness and play-acting of society for what it is, realizes fundamentally that none of it matters on any kind of grand scale, and takes his comforts in food and irritability. He is what we all are, on our worst days, a man totally cowed by the futility of the human project, and the double futility of a realization of his mechanical nature, and having quite the adventure in spite of all that knowledge. His bumbling master, who is good for little else but waxing indignant, checking his very fine watch, and taking snuff, is thoroughly dependent on Jacques, and is sentimentally, one might say neurotically, attached to his philosophical self-delusions, but can't quite make them go in the face of the good-natured fatalism of Jacques. It is precisely the book that the dour philosophy of determinism needed—a raucous and liberating romp that enjoys the unknown ride of life, even as it recognizes the essentially programmed nature of it all. Amidst the imposing and unforgiving Correctness of Hobbes and company, it manages at last some legitimate Joy, needed as much then as now.

Of course, if editing the entire *Encyclopédie*, and writing the first and greatest works to creatively render the living paradoxes of modernist philosophy isn't enough for you, let us not forget that Diderot also revolutionized French theater, elevated craft techniques to a position of general esteem, assembled the basis of the Hermitage's art collection, exposed the cruelty of the convent system in his early novel *The Nun,* warmly supported the American Revolution, inveighed against colonialism in all its forms, invented modern art criticism, and befriended Jean-Jacques Rousseau far longer than most managed to. He is one of the great exceptions to the rule that, to be brilliant, one must be a bit cruel. As creator, philosopher, and human, he was the full flowering of the Enlightenment tradition, who often lived in dire poverty, and never received the flood of titles and positions that fell upon his other *philosophe* colleagues. But he lived happily all the same, a self-contented machine always ready to learn something new, or chat with an old friend come evening.

FURTHER READING

Jacques the Fatalist and His Master is smashing. You need a copy. Order one now. The Penguin edition translated by Michael Henry quite literally changed the entire direction of my life. Then, if you want to know more about Diderot the man, there are two excellent biographies that are commonly available, *Diderot* by Arthur M. Wilson (1957), and *Diderot: A Critical Biography* by P.N. Furbank (1992). As to Diderot's other works, *The Nun* (which originated from a practical joke and ended as a tragic story of the cruelty to human nature perpetrated by the convent system), *The Indiscreet Jewels* (a comedy in which genitalia are given the power to talk, and proceed to tell their tales), *The Letter on the Blind* (featuring a crushing rebuke of God's indifferent cruelty), *D'Alembert's Dream, Rameau's Nephew,* and Diderot's short stories are all readily available in English, along with some selections of his literary and artistic essays. In French, you've got the Diderot volumes in the excellent *Classiques Garnier* series, which includes all manner of texts that have yet to be translated.

The Royal Road to Enlightenment: Frederick the Great

The sun is going down on a gore-soaked battlefield and there, under a field tent, a king in a uniform riddled with bullet holes plays a flute solo of his own devising into the putrescent air. Few images sum up the promise and devastation of the eighteenth century, its capacity for paradox and tragicomedy, as well as this of Prussian monarch Frederick the Great, escaping temporarily from omnipresent carnage through the soothing elegance of artistic expression. He was *the* Enlightened monarch—the patron of Voltaire, Euler, Maupertuis, La Mettrie, and Lagrange—a composer of poems, histories, concerti, and libretti—a religious disbeliever who ran the most tolerant country in Europe. He was also the soldier king whose need to cut a figure on the European stage culminated in two wars that cost the lives of hundreds of thousands of human beings. No monarch worked harder for the wellbeing of his people, and none had a lower opinion of those he ruled. Flute and cannon, plough and verse, all mingle together in the impenetrable figure, the "magnificent enigma," of Frederick the Great.

He was born on January 24, 1712 into a Prussia that had yet to figure itself out. His grandfather was the foppiest king in Europe, a palace-building dandy who wrangled the title of king *in* Prussia out of the Holy Roman Emperor, but not King *of* Prussia. His father was a roughly spherical militarist who collected tall soldiers and ran his country like a regiment. Prussia's sand-fouled soil, manic political borders, and dour Calvinism all combined to make it the State Europe Could Forget. It was the place you could rent some troops from in a pinch, the place you reluctantly traveled *through*

to get to Russia. Even Poland, which wasn't a country anymore by the end of the century, was considered a greater player on the European stage than swampy, industry poor Prussia.

Frederick would change all of that, but not before being twisted and broken by personal horrors. He was a sensitive child in a court that considered nothing so enjoyable as smoking tobacco and drinking tokay in a dingy room to the point of passing out, or, for real sophistication, harassing a few bedraggled boar to death out in the forest. He and his sister Wilhelmina loved music and verse, and fine clothes and all things French. He played the flute and she the lute, and his father disapproved of all of it. He berated and physically beat his son for his "effeminacy," wielding the cane while pathetically demanding to be loved. Frederick learned to retire into himself, to put on a public face of obedience while privately building up a secret library of his favorite French works, especially his beloved Voltaire, and plotting a way to escape the drudgery of the Prussian court.

The last extreme came when his father announced that Frederick was to marry an intellectually dull but solidly German daughter of his friend, the Duke of Brunswick-Bevern. Frederick had his heart set on a double marriage which would give him an English princess and make his favorite sister the Queen of England. He resolved to flee, first to France and then to London, and enlisted the help of his dearest friend, Hans Hermann von Katte. The plot was easily discovered, and Frederick arrested, along with von Katte. Von Katte received a death sentence and, in an act of especial cruelty, Frederick's father ordered that the execution be carried out in

front of Frederick's prison cell, while Frederick was compelled to watch.

At just eighteen years of age, the young crown prince had to watch his best friend beheaded, the body left to fester in the blood-soaked dust. It broke him. The king contemplated execution for Frederick as well, but decided instead to leave him incarcerated for a further three months. When he emerged, Frederick agreed to everything his father demanded. He would marry the insipid German, and become the dutiful son. He would study the arts of statesmanship and tactics, as his father laid them out. With the descent of the executioner's blade, Frederick's two personae, the dreaming philosopher and the hardened cynic, fused. He would carry that contradiction for the rest of his days, to Europe's consternation and Prussia's glory.

Frederick married and, with the freedom from restraint that the marriage brought, proceeded to live life as he saw fit, creating a core of philosophizing free spirits at his Rheinsburg palace. Frederick divided his time between philosophizing, composing, and learning the business of kingship with a liberty and lightness he would never know again. He wrote to his favorite intellectuals, scribbled out reams of poems, mocked religion scandalously, and venerated the classical ideals of the Athenian and Stoic traditions. It was training for the day he would be king, with a nation's resources to devote to the causes of reason and art, and it could not endure.

In 1740, the king died at last, and Frederick assumed the throne just months before the Austrian monarch also passed, leaving his substantial territories to his daughter, Maria Theresa. All of Europe had agreed to respect her right to assume the throne, and none of Europe actually did. The royal corpse was hardly lukewarm before the vultures began to descend, and Frederick was the first among them. His life had been ruined by Austrian scheming, and his father's reign was a series of promises made and forgotten by the haughty Habsburg family. With a crack army and a full war chest courtesy of his father, Frederick was ready to show the Habsburgs what Prussia could do. He descended on their richest province, Silesia, and claimed it as his own while his French allies worked towards their own ends. And then, having attained what he wanted, he promptly jumped back out of the war, leaving the French in the lurch. From that point forward, *unreliable* vied with *brilliant* as the word that summed up Frederick in the European consciousness.

Frederick defies categorization. For every battle where he took fright and fled ignominiously, there are three where he exposed himself repeatedly to intense danger, bullets whizzing through his clothes and killing his steeds under him. For every expression of deep sentiment and duty, there are a dozen cynical utterances of total despair at humanity's capacity for self-enlightenment. Contradiction aside, Frederick easily won this first war, put his new province in his pocket, and proceeded to recreate Athens in the middle of the Prussian swampland. He built Sanssouci, a palace atop a terraced vineyard that was to be his retreat from the world, where he and his philosopher friends would gather and discuss with complete freedom the things of the mind. He invited Voltaire (who would return the favor by attempting to defraud the state hosting him and destabilize its

nascent academic life) and La Mettrie (who died from a paté), two of the most infamous religious critics of their time, the latter an avowed atheist who wrote *Man, a Machine,* the most explicit European text at the time in establishing the purely mechanical nature of human beings. The king even wrote his own tracts about the tangled history of religion and superstition, including an operatic libretto, *Montezuma,* that was set to music by Graun, about the excesses of Catholicism and organized religion generally, which is still performed very occasionally.

He made tolerance the central principle of his state and his philosophy and saw, well before any other figures of the Enlightenment did, that intolerance within humanism was something to be anticipated and avoided, lest those without religion become like those with it. "We know the crimes which religious fanaticism has engendered. Let us take care to keep philosophy free of fanaticism; it should be characterized by moderation," he wrote to Voltaire, and his country was one where Jesuit, atheist, Jew, and Lutheran all had a place so long as they obeyed the laws and made themselves useful.

In the meantime, there was a new culture to build. The Academy of Berlin was revived, and illustrious names added to its roles, including Maupertuis, Algarotti, Euler, and Lagrange. Frederick built, piece by piece, the best orchestra in Europe, featuring at one time CPE Bach, the virtuosic Benda clan, the flautist Johann Quantz, and the composer Carl Heinrich Graun. Frederick's opera, likewise grown from nothing, was also one of the greatest in Europe, offering new compositions performed by continent-class performers every winter, while at Sanssouci itself the king regularly gave

concerts of his own and Quantz's flute concerti. Science, art, philosophy, tolerance, and reasonable laws all converged for that one shining moment before all of Europe decided they'd had quite enough of this Frederick upstart and elected to unite their forces to utterly crush him.

Here in the United States, we know the Seven Years' War as the French-and-Indian War which gained Canada for Britain and made necessary the taxes which would provide the justification of Revolution a decade later. In Europe, they were, quite explicitly, the Smash Frederick wars. Austria, France, Sweden, and Russia all agreed to forget their previous grievances and unite to destroy Prussia's power for good. Only Britain lent aid the besieged monarch, seeing no profit in the strengthening of the Franco-Russo-Austro hands.

By all reckoning, Frederick should have been crushed, and quickly. But he simply refused to be. While the allies were gathering up their resources, he sprung, re-establishing his lines and rounding on army after army, effecting lightning marches to deal now with the French, now with the Austrians, facing off against forces twice his number and regularly winning thanks to his well-drilled cavalry and often revolutionary sense of tactics. He made disastrous mistakes, and was nearly knocked from the game entirely on several occasions, but always bounded back, reformed his army, and staved off defeat another year. For seven long years the marshy provinces of Prussia managed to hold off... basically all of Europe, until finally the Russian tsarina quite obligingly died and her son, a Frederick the Great fanatic, came to the throne and pulled his country's forces out of the war. Frederick, his eastern front secure, dealt a few more blows to the Austrian forces, until peace was at last sued for, and in 1763 Frederick was re-established as ruler of Silesia, and Prussia as the unconquerable rock of Europe.

It had cost much blood. Besides the nearly 200,000 soldiers who had died, the French, Russian, and Croat pillaging and raping of the countryside had destroyed hundreds of towns and as many as another 300,000 lives. Frederick, the flute-playing philosopher who loved peace and reason, stood at the end of the war with a broken if proud nation, possessed by the question of whether it was all morally justifiable. His friends and generals all dead, misery written on the faces of every villager in the contested borderlands, was it worth it?

Frederick was resolved to make sure that it was. He rose at three every morning and set to work, ordering the rebuilding of villages, the recodifying of the laws along modern principles, the draining of marshes, the promotion of industry, and the development of a merit-based bureaucracy, all to make good the hurt he had inflicted on his land during his first heady months as monarch. Seven years of strain and death and emergency had taken their toll—he was physically wrecked and could not see the good of the world through the bloodshed. How could he witness the raped women and burning farms of East Prussia, and still hold onto the hope of man's basic goodness? And yet, he didn't abandon mankind. He pushed every reserve of energy he had into finding ways to help his people. He gave them good food

and what he hoped were good laws, let them think as they would so long as they lived in accord with their neighbors, all while himself experiencing each day a diminution of life's joys.

The loss of his teeth meant that he could no longer play flute, the death of his friends that he no longer had somebody to confide his fears and self-doubts to, and his family were merely waiting around to see him at last gone. In his letters, we see a man in constant pain, aware of his faults, trying to take solace in the philosophy of the Stoics and in leaving behind something that would allow people to treat each other equitably and justly at last. He died in his chair, alone save for his two greyhounds, which are buried next to him today, on a hill, near some grapevines, without worries.

FURTHER READING

Frederick the Great has been my constant companion for the better part of a decade now. Since 2007, Geoff Schaeffer and I have, twice a week, every week, written time-spanning adventures with Frederick at the helm in our webcomic *Frederick the Great: A Most Lamentable Comedy Breaching Time and Space* (available online at www.ftg-comic.com!). In that time, I've gotten to read *a few* Frederick books, and they are all, on the whole, quite good, though most are focused on the military side of his career rather than the intellectual. For the philosopher and writer, I like *Frederick the Great: A Life in Deed and Letters* by Giles MacDonogh. Robert Asprey's *Frederick the Great: The Magnificent Enigma* is another one which does justice to all the different aspects of Frederick. Nancy Mitford and Thomas Carlyle are also fun if you're in the hero worship-y mood. In German, the classics are Franz Kugler's *Geschichte Friedrichs des Grossen* from 1842, and Reinhold Koser's four-volume biography of the same title, completed in 1912. More recently, Johannes Kunisch's *Friedrich der Grosse: Der Koenig und seine Zeit* (2004) is a neat book putting Frederick in his eighteenth-century context while at the same time showing how much he anticipated of modernity.

Trying Herder: The Lost Voice of the Eighteenth Century's Greatest Twenty-First Century Thinker

STRASSBURG, 1772.

HERDER! YOU LOOK LIKE YOU'RE THINKING LANGUAGE-Y THOUGHTS.

HM? NO, I WAS JUST WONDERING WHY OWLS.

WHY OWLS WHAT?

JUST "WHY OWLS?" GENERALLY. BUT LANGUAGE IS TROUBLING TOO...

WHY SO?

SO MUCH OF A WORD'S MEANING IS IN ITS TONAL AND CULTURAL *CONTEXT*, BOTH OF WHICH GET SWALLOWED BY TIME. WHICH MEANS THAT EACH YEAR A LITTLE MORE OF A SENTENCE'S MEANING IS IRREVOCABLY LOST.

BUMMER. SO WHAT THOUGH?

I WONDER WHY GOD WOULD CHOOSE BOOKS FILLED WITH WORDS TO CONVEY HIS MESSAGE, KNOWING THAT, AFTER A FEW HUNDRED YEARS, ONLY THEIR BAREST DEFINITIONS WOULD REMAIN, AND SOMETIMES NOT EVEN THAT?

WHY ENTRUST A MESSAGE SO IMPORTANT TO A CARRIER SO UNRELIABLY ETHEREAL?

DUDE, I KNOW YOU'RE A CLERGYMAN, BUT THERE'S A PRETTY OBVIOUS ANSWER.

HE'S TESTING OUR FAITH?

ORRRR....?

IT'S ALL PART OF A LARGER PLAN?

SURE. WE'VE ALREADY PUT MOSQUITOES, EARTHQUAKES, AND INTERMITTENT SLAVERY IN THAT BOX - WHY NOT THE GROSS INADEQUACY OF RELIGIOUS LANGUAGE TOO?

Of all the crimes a late eighteenth-century German cultural thinker could commit, none carried a stiffer sentence than Not Being Goethe. Klopstock, Möser, Süssmilch, Reimarus, Herder...all names blasted out of our common memory by their proximity to the towering figure of the Weimar poet. And while there probably isn't anybody weeping torrents over the loss of Süssmilch, the obscurity of Johannes Gottfried Herder (1744-1803) is actually rather tragic. Consistently two centuries ahead of his time, his ideas about linguistics and comparative history had to wait until the twentieth century for a rebirth, while his reflections on cognition are shockingly prescient. How was it that such an original and deep thinker became so utterly lost to us?

The real problem is that he wasn't so much lost as dismembered. The Romantics took his stance against Pure Reason, chopped it up into a few ringing phrases, and used it as a part of their more general campaign against the Enlightenment. And so the nineteenth century came to see Herder as a great irrationalist in spite of his many writings praising reason and science as crucial paths to the self-realization of humanity. The twentieth century, when it bothered to notice him at all, saw only his comments about the cultural specificity of language and heralded them as precursors of Quinean relativism, conveniently ignoring the parts of his work which stress the unifying quality of our human cognitive processes.

What has come down to us, then, has been a series of partial Herders hitched to the wagons of fleeting philosophical and cultural movements, caricatures so broadly drawn that they understandably failed to outlive their revivers. The whole Herder is a creature hardly seen in nature before it is set upon and harvested for organs by whatever academic faction happens to be hungry for provenance at the time.

He was born in Mohrungen, East Prussia, a town of about a thousand souls known for the production of cattle and theologians. Shaking the dust of that small town from his boots, he ended up at the tender age of eighteen in Königsberg, which was the place to be for a budding thinker, offering the chance to study not only under the great champion of holism, Johann Georg Hamann, but also an up-and-comer by the name of Immanuel Kant.

His first writings were in the field of literary criticism and flew in the face of pretty much every major school of thought at the time, setting a life-long precedent of pissing off the philosophical establishment. While the Enlightenment thinkers were seeking to find universal laws for drama and aesthetics, Herder came out swinging hard for evaluating each work of drama against the historical standards and practices of its time and culture. Rather than denigrating Shakespeare for not being Voltaire, he argued, oughtn't we consider what his work means in the context of Elizabethan society and concerns? Common sense now, perhaps, but revolutionary stuff coming from the heart of the Enlightenment and its mania for universal systems.

More astounding still are the thoughts he put to paper in response to a Berlin Academy prompt of 1769. The theme was the origin of language, a topic up to that time dominated by two warring schools—the first held firmly to the idea that language must be of divine origin, while the other held that it is already present in animals, evident in the growl of the lowliest town mutt. Herder ran counter to both of these schools, and in the process very nearly created modern linguistic and neural theory in eighteenth-century Prussia.

Language was for Herder a distinctly human phenomenon born from man's unique cognitive practices. It is in the very structure of how we approach and perceive the world. In a move that anticipated discoveries in neuroscience made within the last half century, Herder identified reflection, networking, and plastic association as the hallmarks of human cognitive life.

What separates man from animals, Herder believed, is man's capacity for reflection, for grabbing a passing idea and holding onto it while considering its relation to other facts of the world. He found the root of language in this uniquely human capacity, and in doing so somewhat astoundingly provided us with a definition of the lateral prefrontal cortex and its functions before it had even been discovered. Some poetic turns of phrase aside, his focus on the centrality of reflection belongs solidly in the twenty-first century: "Man manifests reflection when the force of his soul acts in such freedom that, in the vast ocean of sensations which permeates it through all the channels of the senses, it can single out one wave, arrest it, concentrate its attention on it, and be conscious of being attentive. He manifests reflection when, confronted with the vast hovering dream of images which pass by his senses, he can collect himself into a moment of wakefulness and dwell at will on one image, can observe it clearly and more calmly... so that he will know this object is this and not another."

Fast forward 250 years, and the discoveries of neuroscience are just now showing us that the possession of a prefrontal cortex in primates is what allows working memory—holding an idea and considering its connections to others without being externally stimulated to do so—to function and that, further, this is the zone where our linguistic processing modules are found. Positing working memory rather than pure reason as the root of humanity and human language was a stroke of genius too far ahead of its time to succeed, but Herder didn't stop there.

Facing a world that was trying to split human actions into the purely reasonable or emotional, Herder replied that, "If we have grouped certain activities of the soul under certain major designations, such as wit, perspicacity, fantasy, reason, this does not mean that a single act of mind is ever possible in which only wit or only reason is at work; it means no more than that we discern in that act a prevailing share of the abstraction we call wit or reason...if ever a man was able to perform a single act in which he thought totally like an animal, he is *ipso facto* no longer a man in any thing, no longer capable of any human act." It took two and a half centuries to come back to this truth, that you can't wall off parts of the brain from each other. As we've since come to discover, even our simplest acts require the networking of multiple brain centers in exquisite unison crafted by the neural connections determined by genetics and past experience.

The imprint of experience was a theme that Herder would return to repeatedly in his historical and linguistic work. In a move that anticipated Kristeva's semiotic theory, he argued strongly that words must not be considered purely from the point of view of their logical structure, but also in terms of their rhythmic, emotional, and experiential elements. As he rather fancifully put it, "This weary breath—half a sigh—which dies away so movingly on pain-distorted lips, isolate it from its living helpmeets, and

it is an empty draft of air." The sound and rhythm of language, which held so much of the meaning of words in their original contexts, are largely left behind on the printed page, and as we lose touch with the historical situation when our words were formed, so do our own words taste increasingly artificial on our lips. They become the worn-beyond-recognition coins that Nietzsche would make famous a century later.

This was particularly a problem, Herder saw, for his own profession as a preacher

and philosopher. "The most meaningful sacred symbols of every people, no matter how well-adapted to the climate and nation, frequently lose their meaning within a few generations. This should come as no surprise, for this is bound to happen to every language and to every institution that has arbitrary signs as soon as these signs are not frequently compared to their objects through active use...as soon as [priests] lost the meaning of the symbols, they had to become either the silent servants of idolatry or the loquacious liars of superstition. They did become this almost everywhere, not out of any particular propensity to deception, but out of the natural course of things."

Such considerations of the particularity of linguistic and cultural practice made Herder a fierce champion of the right of each nation to find happiness through its own means, to be evaluated on its own terms, and to hold with whatever religious notions made sense in its own language and tradition. He despised colonialism and the forcible religious conversion of native people. He would have none of any historical system which attempted to posit a scale of perfection with modernity sitting regally at the top. "No one in the world feels the weakness of generalizing more than I... Who has noticed how inexpressible the individuality of one human being is—how impossible it is to express distinctly an individual's distinctive characteristics? Since this is the case, how can one possibly survey the ocean of entire peoples, times, and countries, and capture them in one glance, one feeling, or one word? What a lifeless, incomplete phantom of a word it would be! You must first enter the spirit of a nation in order to empathize completely with even one of its thoughts or deeds." Just as Shakespeare was not Euripides Done Wrong, neither is India just Ancient Greece Done Wrong. To posit a happiest or best civilization is to establish a scale of comparison where there are in fact just people working after whatever satisfaction that their situation can afford them.

And lest his contemporaries believe they had a real chance to fully understand and therefore judge a culture by reading about it in an open and empathetic spirit, Herder gleefully yanked the rug away by pointing out the utter hopelessness of genuine translation: "Those varied significations of one root that are to be traced and reduced to their origin in its genealogical tree are interrelated by no more than vague feelings, transient side associations, and perceptional echoes which arise from the depth of the soul and can hardly be covered by rules. Furthermore, their interrelations are so specifically national, so much in conformity with the manner of thinking and seeing of the people, of the inventor, in a particular country, in a particular time, under particular circumstances, that it is exceedingly difficult for a Northerner and Westerner to strike them right." You will always miss something, and there is no way of knowing whether that something was insignificant or was, after all, the most important part of the concept you were trying to nail down.

Which brings us to George Orwell. Because, not content with establishing a network theory of cognition, a semiotic theory of language, and a comparative approach to historiography and literature centuries before their time, he also analyzed the role of linguistic association in mass politics before mass politics really even existed. Take a look at this, written in 1772:

"What is it that works miracles in the assemblies of people, that pierces hearts, and upsets souls? Is it intellectual speech and metaphysics? Is it similes and figures of speech? Is it art and coldly convincing reason? If there is to be more than blind frenzy, much must happen through these; but everything? And precisely this highest moment of blind frenzy, through what did it come about?—Through a wholly different force! These tones, these gestures, those simple melodious continuities, this sudden turn, this dawning voice-what more do I know?—They all ... accomplish a thousand times more than truth itself... The words, the tone, the turn of this gruesome ballad or the like touched our souls when we heard it for the first time in our childhood with I know not what host of connotations of shuddering, awe, fear, fright, joy. Speak the word, and like a throng of ghosts those connotations arise of a sudden in their dark majesty from the grave of the soul: They obscure inside the word the pure limpid concept that could be grasped only in their absence."

Somehow, sitting in an autocratic Prussian state almost devoid of mature political institutions, Herder managed to piece together the notion of subliminal messaging and its potential use in mass media politicking. Politics as the art of using tone and rhythm to recall primal past experiences and therefore elicit the desired present emotions quite aside from the actual content of the words being spoken.

This isn't to say that Herder was always so prescient or revolutionary. His answer for the existence of suffering is little different than the colossally unconvincing argument St. Augustine trotted out thirteen centuries earlier. But these halfhearted gestures pale next to the monumental leaps of imagination with which he enriched the late eighteenth century and, if we are willing, our own. Many of his ideas we have since rediscovered, but loaded down with such onerous and generally unenlightening jargon (I'm looking at you, Carl Jung) that the scope and profundity of those ideas have been drastically and tragically narrowed. A return to the source is in order, the whole Herder, often fanciful, sometimes deliciously naïve, but never more relevant than the present.

It's Beginning to Loki a Lot Like Christmas: A Cartoon History of Humanism Holiday Special!

Whether to explain evil in the world, or just to add a splash of narrative tension to an otherwise pedestrian parable, theistic religions seem unable to forego the subversive pleasure of creating compelling Bad Guys. Tricksters who are supposed to represent the summit of greed and malevolence but yet who retain our interest and become our heroes in a way that their monotonically virtuous counterparts can't. Lucifer, the laughing Lord of Hell who is the secular patron saint of intellectual rebellion, blood-soaked Kali, whose primal violence is tinged with compassion, and always and forever, Loki, the grand god of mischief.

For a century and a half now, Loki has reigned as our favorite polytheistic foil to religious pretensions. In his persona of Loge, he judges the vain gods and their haughty attempts to build a self-serving paradise in Richard Wagner's *Der Ring des Nibelungen*. While Wotan and his family march into their newly constructed Walhalla, bought through blood and deception, Loge lingers outside, offering the final word: "Ihrem Ende eilen sie zu,"—They hasten to their end, he sneers while fantasizing about wiping them out in a grand conflagration before pulling himself back to reality at last with a very Lokian shrug—"Bedenken will ich's. Wer weiss, was ich tun?" I'll think on it—who knows what I'll end up doing? Loki is a mystery, even to himself. He sympathizes with the Rhine Maidens whom the gods ran roughshod over, and mocks his divine brethren with delicious malice as they droop and slacken from the lack of Freia's golden apples. Between the *Ring*'s thick-skulled heroes, blustering dwarves, and impotently flailing deities, Loge stands out as the sharp voice of reason, the audience's representative and touchstone, pushing the gods on through guile and deceit to their ultimate, well-deserved destruction, their elaborate power broken on the rocks of absolute love.

Wagner took *a few* liberties with the Norse sagas when constructing the *Ring,* changing characters around to make events overlap, and suffusing the whole thing with his own ideas about redemptive sacrifice. But the character of Loki is more or less on the money, his destructive nobility a fair representation of the Norsemen's own conflicted accounts of Loki's part in the pantheon. In one ancient story, a peasant couple are desperate to hide their son from the giant Skrymsli. They apply to Odin, who gives it his best shot, fails, and leaves. Then to Hoenir, who also tries, also fails, and also leaves. Then, finally, desperate, they call on Loki, who tries to hide the child by disguising him as an egg in the womb of a fish. When Skrymsli finds the egg, instead of giving up, as the other gods had done, Loki tells the child to run and erects a trap for the pursuing giant, finally subduing and slaughtering it, securing the child's freedom. Loki is the god who kept trying, who would use his last resource in the pursuit of what he promised to do, while the higher gods couldn't be bothered with anything more than their first efforts.

He was the jealous villain responsible for the death of Baldr, most beloved of the gods, but at the same time he was the oddly heroic savior who was willing to get impregnated by a wild stallion to protect the sun and moon.

Perhaps that story needs some filling out. And what's Christmas for if not to sit around, besotted by nog, and listen to tales of Norse gender/species swapping?

So, the gods wanted to build a palace to house their splendor, but the only architect willing to undertake the task demanded as payment Freia, the sun, and the moon. Odin was all, "Dude, palaces are cool, but come on... the sun?" but then Loki convinced him to strike a deal to the effect that payment would only be offered if the palace were built in thirty days, using only one horse to do the work. Seemed like a good plan, only the architect had a wicked-good horse, and the palace was in danger of finishing easily on schedule. So, Loki did the only thing he could reasonably do. He changed himself into a mare, went to the building site, shook his/her alluring horse nethers a bit, and then took off into the forest, with the architect's workhorse in hot pursuit, only stopping with the coming of morning and thus the end of the period allotted by the bet. The workhorse got it on with she-horse-Loki, and Loki would eventually give birth to Sleipnir, Odin's eight-footed mount. If there is a Norse reward for Taking One For the Team, Loki wins it easily, and I didn't even tell the tale of the time that he tied his testicles to the beard of a goat to try and coax laughter out of a vengeful Skadi.

Everything about Loki is divine contradiction, humanity's tortured self-assessment painted in epic strokes. As the husband of Glut, he was the god of the hearth, and the being responsible for creating mankind's manifold passions, and therefore the source of our entire emotional life. Yet, as husband of Angur-boda, he was the father of Hela, goddess of death, the Midgard serpent, and the wolf Fenris. The gods loved him for his humor, and his ability to always come through in the end with some impossible scheme for victory. And they hated him for slaying Baldr and then preventing his return to the world of the living. He was Thor's beloved companion, and ended his days lashed with the guts of his children to a stone beneath a perpetually poison-leaking snake, attended by one of his wives by way of mercy, there to remain until Ragnarok. The classic image of Sigyn, standing with a bowl raised above Loki's head to catch the dropping snake venom, only leaving her husband's side to empty the bowl and

thence to renew her station, is one of the great pictures in the mythological canon, a piece of wisdom from our Norse friends that nobody is beyond Love, and nobody need resign themselves to being alone. Put next to the Christian willingness to chuck entire continents into the pits of everlasting torture, it is little wonder that we can't stop telling stories of Loki and his doomed guile.

Which brings us to Loki as he is known now, as a comic book super villain. First appearing in 1962 in Marvel's *Journey Into Mystery* #85, he was a typical Stan Lee villain—jealous and power-obsessed, given to making grandiose speeches, and foiled a little *too* easily by his hammer-wielding brother, Thor. (One time, Thor defeats him with popcorn. Really.) But Loki and Thor both have evolved over the years, and the two of them are, now, the focal point of Marvel's biggest storylines involving the dubious worth of the race of gods, and the basic nature of goodness. While Thor waged war against Gorr, the God Butcher, Loki was given a chance to start over life

again as a child, knowing everything of his past, of what people expect him to become, fighting against the compulsions of his nature, and wrestling in the grey areas of morality and determinism in a way unthinkable to the cackling Loki of the '60s. In the world of comic books, if not yet completely in the world of film, Loki is again who he has ever been: the most human of the gods, a little vain, a little deceptive, and always struggling to navigate the space between good intentions and natural selfishness.

A thousand years ago, Norsemen listened to the crackle of flames, and told each other "Hear, Loki is beating his children again." As a god, Loki was accessible, understandable in a way that Odin or Baldr could never be. He was the focal point for real moral questioning, and in the contradictory pages of the Eddas devoted to him there is written a whole people's twisted self-congratulation and thrumming doubt. They couldn't quite figure out what, ultimately, to do with this slippery god, and I suppose we never shall either.

And so the stories go on.

FURTHER READING

For classic Loki, Snorri Sturluson's twelfth-century *The Prose Edda* is a good place to start, or for a more modern collecting of Loki lore, H.A. Guerber's *Myths of the Norsemen From the Eddas to the Sagas* is a nice, very readable, accounting of some of the greatest tales of Norse mythology. For Wagner's Loki, there is none better than Gerhard Stolze's interpretation on the old Herbert von Karajan recording of *Das Rheingold*. Alternately cunning and noble, mocking and sympathetic, it might be my favorite operatic performance, period. Some people can't stand it. Those people are wrong. Then, for Marvel Loki, Kieron Gillen's recent reimagining of the character, beginning in *Journey Into Mystery* 622, is a great hopping-on point, and the tradition continues strong with twenty-something Loki in Al Ewing's run of *Loki: Agent of Asgard*, available at a friendly comic book vendor near you!

Fear not, the Adventure Continues!

Dave's meanderings through time are far from done, so do join us for Volume II, where our intrepid hero evolves with Charles Darwin, hitchhikes with Douglas Adams, busts spirit mediums with Harry Houdini, fixes neurotic Victorians with George Eliot, peers too long into the eyes of monsters with Friedrich Nietzsche, and gets thoroughly pragmatic with Richard Rorty! Coming SOON!

CPSIA information can be obtained
at www.ICGtesting.com
Printed in the USA
LVOW02s0448101116
512406LV00006B/146/P

9 780931 779701